MOTHER MARY
SPEAKS TO US

MOTHER MARY
SPEAKS TO US

Brad Steiger
and
Sherry Hansen Steiger

A DUTTON BOOK

DUTTON
Published by the Penguin Group
Penguin Books USA Inc., 375 Hudson Street,
New York, New York 10014, U.S.A.
Penguin Books Ltd, 27 Wrights Lane,
London W8 5TZ, England
Penguin Books Australia Ltd, Ringwood,
Victoria, Australia
Penguin Books Canada Ltd, 10 Alcorn Avenue,
Toronto, Ontario, Canada M4V 3B2
Penguin Books (N.Z.) Ltd, 182–190 Wairau Road,
Auckland 10, New Zealand

Penguin Books Ltd, Registered Offices:
Harmondsworth, Middlesex, England

First published by Dutton, an imprint of Dutton Signet,
a division of Penguin Books USA Inc.
Distributed in Canada by McClelland & Stewart Inc.

First Printing, November, 1996
10 9 8 7 6 5 4 3 2 1

 REGISTERED TRADEMARK—MARCA REGISTRADA

LIBRARY OF CONGRESS CATALOGING-IN-PUBLICATION DATA:

Steiger, Brad.
    Mother Mary speaks to us / Brad Steiger and Sherry Hansen Steiger.
        p.   cm.
    Includes bibliographical references.
    ISBN 0-525-94125-8
    1. Mary, Blessed Virgin, Saint—Apparitions and miracles—History—20th century.
    2. Mary, Blessed Virgin, Saint—Cult—History—20th century.   I. Steiger, Sherry
    Hansen.   II. Title.
BT650.S74   1996
232.91'7—dc20   96-19382
                                                                     CIP

Printed in the United States of America
Set in Galliard
Designed by Leonard Telesca

Contents

CHAPTER I

This Is the Age of Mary

On November 10, 1991, Theresa Lopez, a thirty-one-year-old mother of three, saw the Virgin Mary at the Mother Cabrini shrine on a hillside west of Denver, Colorado. According to Theresa, this was the eighth time that Mother Mary had appeared to her in an eighteen-month period. She described Mary as life-size, wearing a pink gown with a gold crown and a veil. The Blessed Mother was enveloped in light, and before she vanished, she kissed Theresa on the forehead and asked her to urge all people to have more faith in God.

As word of Theresa Lopez's sightings spread, thousands flocked to the shrine, including many seeking healings. Theresa told the *Denver Post* on November 22, 1991, that many other women had testified to her that they, too, had seen Mary.

Sister Marie-Danielle, a twenty-five-year-old nun in L'Avenir, Quebec, has reported daily visitations from the Blessed Mother for several years. The sister states that Mary gives warning of terrible ordeals that will face the world if people do not return to God.

On August 22, 1992, Sister Marie-Danielle said that Mother Mary appeared surrounded by angels and implored her to urge people to pray for peace. Mary said that she has the power to stop the global "chastisements" that will be starting soon—but only if people "would listen and pray."

When the Blessed Mother came to twenty-seven-year-old Elizabeth Weaver of Kansas City, Missouri, in 1993 and told her to build a statue in her image, Elizabeth got her friend Philip Rustici to assist her, and the two began working almost around the clock to comply with Mary's request.

Three weeks later, when the life-size statue of Mary was placed in the newly constructed grotto in Elizabeth's front lawn, the Blessed Mother appeared in person to thank her.

Elizabeth said that Mary smiled at her. "I will never forget it. She was so beautiful! And her eyes! I'll never forget those eyes!"

There is a grassroots revival of faith in Mother Mary that is taking place worldwide. Sincere men and women are undergoing compelling personal encounters with Mary in private homes, in churches, and in open fields. For whatever reasons, our very planet seems to be crying out for the kind of succor, love, and peace that only a Holy Mother can provide.

"We seem to be doing a terrible job of living up to the Gospel," said Mark Miravalle of Franciscan University in Stuebenville, Ohio. "We need some maternal nagging."

In 1978, Annie Kirkwood, a vocational nurse and mother, began receiving messages from Mother Mary. When Annie protested that she "wasn't even Catholic," the Blessed Mary replied, "Neither am I."

Mary explained to Annie that she was giving messages to individuals of all faiths all over the world, often with appearances and manifestations in the sky to attract large numbers of people. Annie had been selected to relay certain messages, Mother Mary said, because she was a simple and seeking soul.

In 1991, Annie Kirkwood published *Mary's Message to*

the World, a collection of the Blessed Mother's communications that she had received over a three-year period. The book has sold over 350,000 copies, thus reflecting once again a collective need for cosmic mother love and "maternal nagging."

Attendance Soars at Mother Mary's Shrines Throughout the World

Millions of worshipers of all ages are flocking to Mary's many shrines, and the adoration of the Queen of Heaven is rising to an extraordinary level.

- At Lourdes, the best known of France's 937 pilgrimage shrines, annual attendance has risen to 5.5 million.
- Lourdes Grotto in Covent, Louisiana, is a replica of the famous healing shrine in France. In recent years, hundreds of medical miracles have occurred within the shrine's stone walls to those who seek a benevolent sign from Mother Mary.
- In Emittsburg, Maryland, the oldest of forty-three major Marian sites in the United States, the National Shrine Grotto of Our Lady of Lourdes is visited by over a half million people a year.
- Attendance at the Our Lady of Fatima shrine in Washington, New Jersey, has nearly doubled in the past few years.
- After Pope John Paul II paid a visit to the shrine in Knock, Ireland, in 1979, attendance has steadily climbed. In 1986 an international airport was opened at Knock to accommodate 1.5 million people each year.
- When John Paul II made his second visit to Fatima, Portugal, in 1990, he attracted one million devotees. This shrine, where Mary appeared to three children in 1917, regularly draws a steady number of 4.5 million pilgrims a year.

- Before the civil war broke out in former Yugoslavia, more than ten million pilgrims had made the journey to the mountain village of Medjugorje, where Mother Mary imparted messages to six young people in 1981.

Father Roman Schaefer, a Fort Lauderdale priest and a retired air force chaplain, has twice visited Medjugorje.

"Basically, Mother Mary's message is positive," he said. "It is to pray. Prayer can bring peace and move mountains."

We Are Now in the True Age of Mother Mary

"This is the true age of Mary," declared one of the spiritual advisers at the Our Lady of Fatima shrine. "Look around us. We have wars, threats of war, drugs, rampant crime, and a thousand other problems. Men and women are looking frantically for help. In Mother Mary they are sure to find help."

In the 1970s, we learned that Mrs. Janet Bord of London, England, was making an extensive study of the appearance of religious apparitions throughout the world. Through correspondence we asked her which religious figures seemed to manifest the most often. In her reply Mrs. Bord stated: "So far in my research, the Virgin Mary seems to appear the most often, or rather, the female figure that is identified as her. Other traditional saints also appear."

Ann Matter, a specialist in the history of Christianity at the University of Pennsylvania, says that this is the most active age of devotion to Mother Mary, not the twelfth century or the ninth century, but "right now.

"The interest has been building for the past one hundred fifty years, with more and more reports of visions of Mary in more and more places," Ms. Matter said.

Mother Mary and her attending angels have been seen in places as varied as Betania, Venezuela; Cuapa, Nicaragua; Akita, Japan; Damascus, Syria; San Nicholas,

Argentina; Cairo, Egypt; Naju, Korea; and Hrouchiv, Ukraine.

Pope John Paul Embraces Mother Mary's Unifying Power

In 1958, when John Paul II was Bishop Karol Wojtyla of Krakow, Poland, he had a golden *M* for Mary embroidered on his robes and chose as his motto "All Yours," referring not to Christ but to Mother Mary.

In May 1981, after he had been named Pope John Paul II, he was shot by a Turkish radical while riding in a white Jeep in St. Peter's Square. He was still recovering from his wounds when he visited the Basilica of Our Lady of Fatima to give thanks to Mary for saving his life.

Giving full credit to Mary for intervening on his behalf, John Paul II said, in December 1981, "I have seen the extraordinary maternal protection that showed itself to be more powerful than the homicidal bullets."

The pope's faith is rooted firmly in the famed Marian prophecies at Fatima, and he felt that it was no coincidence that the assassination attempt had occurred on May 13, the sixty-fourth anniversary of the day when three devout little children tending sheep in a field near Lisbon, Portugal, first saw the Blessed Mother.

Ever since he became pope, John Paul II has made Mother Mary's unifying power a centerpiece of his earthly mission. He has visited numerous Marian shrines, and he is heard to invoke the Madonna's aid in nearly every prayer he utters.

Mary Brings about the End of Communist Tyranny

Along with millions of others, Pope John Paul II has proclaimed his firm belief that it was Mother Mary who

brought about the end of communism in Russia, thus ful-
filling a prophetic pronouncement made to one of the children at Fatima.

Even while the atheistic philosophy held millions captive
in the former Soviet Union and other countries controlled
by communism, the Blessed Mother remained active. In his
book *Russia Will Be Converted*, James Mafret provided
such accounts of appearances by Mary:

- In 1947 in Italy, at the Tre Fontane, a communist
  sympathizer encountered the apparition of an angel-
  like form that others regarded as the Virgin Mary.
  Thousands of people visited the spot, and many com-
  munists were converted to Roman Catholicism.
- In 1948, Liaret, a local secretary of the Communist
  Party, was standing by a roadside when he saw a tall
  figure he later described as a "lady in light."
- In Trieste in 1948, a young girl was said to have beheld a beautiful lady who told her to return to the
  same spot every day for fifteen days. After having received visions on each of these successive days, the girl
  was presented with the materialization of seven perfect rose petals. It is claimed that the petals did not
  fade or lose their fragrance. It is also said that a
  botanist declared that the petals could not have come
  from an ordinary Earth rose.

Mother Mary Nurtures the Seed of All Humankind

Many observers of the spiritual scene believe that the
frequent appearances of the Virgin Mary over the past hundred and fifty years have to do with the Second Coming of
Christ—or, as the less orthodox might phrase it, the giving
of Cosmic Consciousness to the entire race. St. Louis Mary
de Montfort, a Catholic scholar and writer of the eigh-
teenth century, said: "In the second coming of Jesus, Mary

has to be made known and revealed by the Holy Ghost, in order that, through her, Jesus Christ may be made known, loved, and served."

Some years ago, Nada-Yolanda, a well-known psychic-sensitive and channel who lived in Miami, Florida, said that she had received the following message from Mary:

> I, Mary, am the teacher, the example from which the seed [the message] comes forth. Therefore, manifestations of my work and teachings have to come forth prior to the teachings of the Son of God. . . . I have demonstrated fertility and willingness in the minds of men to receive the message of the Second Coming. . . . The Second Coming is literal as well as spiritual, for the individual as well as for the race."

On another occasion, Nada-Yolanda stated that her master teacher brought forth this additional message:

> Mary represents the subconscious or the mold in which all things are gestated. . . . She is the mother in which the seed does grow. She represents that aspect of the God consciousness as Jesus represents the male, or the active, force. . . . She represents the nourishing part of God's seed, always remembering that each one is representative and a part of the whole. . . .
>
> The role of Mary at this time is the same as it was during the life of Jesus. She nurtured the seed for nine months—and many years, of course, after his birth—as the physical mother. But she is also nurturing the seed of humankind by her special work in the etheric for the last two thousand years—and she will continue until all people are brought into Christ-conscious awareness.

Mary Calls upon Humanity to Mend Its Ways and Prepare for a Global Cleansing

In 1978, Alexander Solzhenitsyn, the Russian Nobel prize winner expelled from the Soviet Union after years of persecution and detention, told a Harvard University audience that even though the West may have achieved great strides in providing civil rights to its citizens, its sense of responsibility to God and society had grown dimmer and dimmer. Such an attitude, he pointed out, did not admit the "intrinsic evil in man" and perceived no higher goal than earthly happiness.

"We have lost the concept of a supreme, complete entity with which to restrain our passions and our irresponsibility," he continued. "We have placed too much hope in politics and social reforms, only to find that we were being deprived of our most precious possession, our spiritual life. It is trampled by the party mob in the East, by the commercial one in the West."

Those revelators who have seen the Blessed Mother appear before them have often been given sermons and messages that are certainly in harmony with Alexander Solzhenitsyn's warnings of ignoring the "intrinsic evil" in humankind and his admonition to regain "the concept of a supreme, complete entity." Mary is concerned with the horrible mess that humankind has made of the planet, and she calls upon all humanity to right itself and mend its ways before an impending time of global cleansing and judgment catches it unaware. Of course, her messages are filled with words of peace and unconditional love, but on some occasions Mary's messages are harsh, direct, and tinged with threats of punishment.

A sampler of admonitions from Mother Mary to her visionaries include such statements as the following:

Immaculate Conception at Lourdes, 1858: "Penitence! Penitence! Penitence! You're to pray to God for sinners.

Go and kiss the ground in penance for the conversion of sinners."

Mother of God to Clemente, Palmar de Troya, Spain, April 25, 1971: "Many times I have told you, 'Obey your priests,' but now I tell you, 'Obey your pastors in that which is fundamental. . . . Many will say, 'Obey the hierarchy,' but I will be speaking with my children in warning them of the deviations, and thus I will pastor them.'"

Lucia dos Santos, Fatima, Portugal, 1961: "It is already time that each one of us accomplishes holy deeds of his own initiative and reforms his life according to Our Lady's appeal. . . . She told me that when the other means of salvation are exhausted and despised by men, She is giving us the last anchor of salvation, that is the Holy Virgin in person."

Our Lady of Carmel, Garabandal, Spain, October 18, 1961, interpreted by the four young girls to whom the Holy Mother appeared: "We must do much penance and make many sacrifices. We must often visit the blessed Sacrament. But above all we must be very good, for if we are not, we will be punished. . . .

"As the punishment which we deserve for the sins of the world are great, the miracle must also be a great one. Our Lady has promised that all mankind will receive a warning from Heaven. The warning comes directly from God and will be visible to the whole world from any place where anyone may happen to be. It . . . will be seen and felt by everyone, believer and unbeliever alike."

Our Lady of Carmel, Garabandal, Spain, November 13, 1965, received by Conchita: "The Blessed Virgin Mary told me that Jesus does not send the punishment in order to distress us, but in order to help us and reproach us because we pay no attention to Him. And the warning will be sent in order to purify us for the miracle in which

He will show us His great love, and in order that we may fulfill the message."

Mother Mary to Oierina, Gilli, Italy, 1974: "The times are getting worse. For many hundreds of years I have come down to many places throughout the world, time and time again."

Queen of the Holy Rosary, Necedah, Wisconsin, May 30, 1950: "Remember my child, that the time is coming. Sorrow and slaughter of my children will be worse than ever in history. It grieves Me to see innocent children, the sick, and the poor destroyed because of greed and desire for power by a few nations' leaders. That is why I say, pray, pray. Give this message to the people, for prayers only will save the destruction of this world."

Blessed Mother to Matous Lasuta, Czechoslovakia, 1958: "Chastisements can be avoided or made lighter by prayer, saying the rosary, penance, and good works."

Mother Mary to Sister Agnes Sasagawa Katsuka, Japan. From 1973 to 1976 a statue of Mother Mary wept tears or blood over a hundred times, and Sister Agnes received many messages of the coming chastisement directed toward the planet: "It will be a punishment greater than the Deluge, such as one has never seen before. Fire will fall from the sky and shall wipe out a great part of humanity, the good as well as the bad. Confidence in me will save."

Blessed Mother to the Italian mystic Elena Leonardi in the 1970s: "The Earth will tremble in a most frightful way, and all humanity will stagger. An unforeseen fire will descend over the whole earth, and a greater part of humanity will be destroyed."

Our Lady, Veronica Lueken, Bayside, New Jersey, about June 1970: "There are many evils throughout your world now that have been created by man in his arrogance and pride. Technology and science of man have promoted diabolical machines for the destruction of mankind.

"My children, unless you make amends, make atonement, do penance, and sacrifice for the sins of mankind, you will be subjected to many trials and chastisements."

Mother Mary to Annie Kirkwood, Carrollton, Texas, December 27 and 31, 1992: "Remember—these changes are good. They bring a cleansing. When everyone is dismayed, you will feel joy, hope, and peace. . . . Not only will the weather be changing, but so will people. They will find out what is of value are the issues of the mind and the heart. The things of this world are corruptible; they perish. What you have in your mind and heart never leaves you. . . .

"Along with the destruction come the seeds of a new beginning. . . . Through it all you will remember always that you are loved. Remember, this is good, necessary, and needed. I am with you daily."

We Are All Potential Mystics

In this book you will find few encounters with Mother Mary that have occurred to leading theologians, learned professors of philosophy, or august members of the religious hierarchy. It would seem that Mary most often favors appearing to children and to rather ordinary men and women. In a number of cases she has manifested to people who were previously almost militantly irreligious.

Dr. Walter Houston Clark, professor emeritus of Andover Theological Seminary, is not at all surprised that revelatory experiences, such as those in which Mother Mary manifests to relay messages, often come to the irreligious. "Such occurrences testify to the fact that we are all basically religious, whether we acknowledge it or not," he told us.

Dr. Clark went on to suggest that conventional religious beliefs may actually militate against such experiences through

closing minds and fostering repressions by dogmatic theological beliefs.

"In our theological institutions," he explained, "religion
is studied rationally and externally. The theological and ecclesiastical mind therefore becomes exceedingly critical and
suspicious of nonrational perceptions and tends to approach religion exclusively in an external way. The nonrational, revelatory experience becomes a threat, because it
is not understood and cannot be controlled."

While Dr. Clark made it clear that he would not banish
the rational approach to religion or religious institutions,
he did feel that too many orthodox traditionalists had
nearly forgotten the roots of religion, "which are mystical,
ecstatic, and revelatory in nature."

In his opinion, it is often the common ordinary person
and sometimes the humble religious believer "who is open-
minded enough to be unfettered by such restrictions and so
is free to experience revelation."

Dr. Clark added that the kind of revelation experience
that had most impressed him in recent years has been that
which has sprung from a greatly deepened religious sensitivity of a religious nature. Such a sensitivity, in his view,
leads often to a greatly lessened valuation on external and
material values in exchange for a strengthened valuation
of the nonrational and a heightened compassion with its
concern for others and for nature.

"I fully agree with William James's statement in his
Varieties of Religious Experience to the effect that personal
religion has its origin in the mystical experience of the individual," Dr. Clark said.

"Succinctly, James expressed my position for me when he
wrote in a letter to a friend: 'The mother sea and fountain-
head of all religions lie in the mystical experiences of the individual. . . . All theologies and ecclesiasticisms are secondary
growths superimposed.'

"I believe that all people are potential mystics, just as
each one of us is a potential poet, mystic, artist, or ecstatic," Dr. Clark continued. "This hunger for the expression

of the nonrational is sleeping within all of us. It goes beyond those valid needs of food, clothing, and shelter that keep our bodies alive. Nonrational and intangible values keep us alive by giving meaning to life, and whether consciously or unconsciously and though suppressed by the priority of material needs in our society, a sensitivity to them always has the possibility of being awakened by the proper stimuli. The longer this sensitivity is neglected or starved, the more spontaneous and forcefully it is expressed when it surfaces."

The Mary Miracle

In his book *The Mary Miracle,* Dr. Jack Hayford, senior pastor of the Church on the Way in Van Nuys, California, tells us that the miracle of Mary reminds us that God himself has chosen no beginning point for His wonder workings apart from human beings:

> In Mary, He demonstrated His readiness and willingness to work through an imperfect human vessel. . . . As amazing as is God's will to come from heaven to earth, an even more transcending grace is manifest in His choice to reveal Himself through the fabric and frame of humankind. . . .
>
> Mary was the first person to experience . . . being chosen, of becoming a vehicle of redemption's fullest and highest expression of grace. . . .
>
> God's redemptive promise was brought *to* her, to grow *in* her, to be delivered *through* her, to change the world *around* her.

Dr. Hayford stresses that the "Mary Miracle" sets in motion a most wonderful process. By choosing Mary, a "mere human vessel" as a physical means through which He might unfold His "wonder working" toward humankind, God thereby revealed "His willingness to bring His promises to nest in fallen human vessels." If the inhabitants of Earth will but open themselves to God's grace, "He is ready to change their world—*through them*! To see and to grasp this is to pave the way for the Mary miracle to occur over and over again."

CHAPTER 2

The Appearances of Mother Mary

Although we have received regular reports of visitations of Mother Mary from around the world, we should make it clear at the outset that the Roman Catholic hierarchy officially recognizes only seven appearances of Mary:

Guadalupe, Mexico: In 1531, an Indian named Juan Diego saw Mother Mary four times and was given a miraculously created serape as evidence of her heavenly visitation.

Paris, France: The Holy Mother appeared to a nun in 1830 and asked her to fashion a medal to commemorate the Immaculate Conception.

La Salette, France: A weeping, sorrowful Mary manifested to two peasant children on September 19, 1846, and instructed them to do penance for their sins.

Lourdes, France: Identifying herself as the Immaculate Conception, Mary appeared eighteen times to fourteen-year-old Bernadette Soubrious between February 11 and July 16, 1858. The waters of the miraculous spring that appeared according to Mary's promise are world famous for their healing powers.

Fatima, Portugal: Mother Mary appeared to three children near here, instructing them to say their rosary frequently. During her six visits between May 13 and October 13, 1917, Mary issued a number of prophecies, many of which are said to be held secret by the Vatican.

Beauraling, Belgium: Between November 29, 1932, and January 3, 1933, five children at a convent school experienced a remarkable thirty-three encounters with Mother Mary in the school garden.

Banneaux, Belgium: Mother Mary appeared to an eleven-year-old girl eight times between January 15 and March 2, 1933, in the garden of her parents' humble cottage.

So much for the Vatican-approved encounters with Mother Mary. There are a number of other visions of Mary that have been highly publicized and may be better known than many of those on the approved list:

Garabandal, Spain: A series of two thousand ecstatic visions of Mother Mary began for four children one Sunday after Mass in 1961. The visitations continued until 1965 and produced numerous prophecies and astonishing miracles.

Zeitoun, Egypt: As many as a million witnesses may have glimpsed the figure of the glowing Madonna standing, kneeling, or praying beside a cross on the roof of St. Mary's Coptic Church. Miraculous cures manifested among the pilgrims from 1968 to 1971.

Medjugorje, Yugoslavia: In 1981, six children saw Mother Mary holding the infant Jesus near the village. The holy figure appeared on an almost daily basis for five months, leaving behind a continuing legacy of miraculous healings.

Bayside, New York: From 1970 to the present day, the "Bayside Seeress," Veronica Lueken, issues pronouncements from Mother Mary against the spiritual abuses of contemporary society.

The Inspired Visions of Tjsje Peerdeman

Tjsje Peerdeman had her initial vision one Saturday evening in 1918, when she was just thirteen years old and was coming home from her first confession.

The Dutch teenager had made a confession filled with accounts of childish misdeeds, which had been magnified in their seriousness by her extreme piety. Tjsje's confessor, Father Joseph Frehe, recognized the girl's extraordinarily devout attitude and demeanor as he heard a recitation of minor transgressions that she conscientiously feared might truly be wrongful acts.

Later, suffused with a marvelous sense of absolution for her long list of supposed sins, Tjsje was heading for her home when her attention was caught by a strange yet marvelous light in the doorway of an old storehouse. As the teenager stood mesmerized, a figure of a beautiful woman appeared in the mysterious glow.

The woman's loveliness was of a celestial, unearthly quality. Could it really be the Blessed Mother? Tjsje fell to her knees in supplication and crossed herself. It most surely appeared to be the Holy Mother Mary.

The lovely woman said nothing, only smiled, and seemed to indicate with a beatific motion of her head that Tjsje should continue on her way home.

When Tjsje confided the wonderful, unearthly experience to her older sister Gesina, she did not receive a warm reception.

"Hush up, Tjsje, and please don't trouble me with such ridiculous tales," Gesina snapped at her. "And don't repeat such nonsense to Father—or he'll thrash you!"

Tjsje respected her sister's admonition. Since Mama had passed away, Gesina had been left to care for the three younger girls. To obey her was as if she was obeying Mama.

And she knew Gesina was correct in her warning about not telling their father of the appearance of the holy lady. Papa was a practical textile merchant who observed the practices of the church when it best suited him, but who had little time for those people who claimed to have experienced mystical enlightenment.

Tjsje told no one of the beautiful woman's first visit, but when the lovely Madonna appeared to her a second and a third time, she did write down the details of each manifestation in her diary.

While she kept her word to Gesina to tell no one, Tjsje did, of course, confess the otherworldly visitations to Father Frehe. She was astonished when he demanded that she turn the diary over to his keeping.

"I must have that diary, girl," Father Frehe told her after her confession. "You must go home and bring the diary back to me straight away."

Sadly but obediently Tjsje brought the diary to Father Frehe, then stood by with tears streaking her cheeks as the priest methodically tore out the pages and ceremoniously crumpled them into small, tight balls before throwing them into the waste basket in his office.

Tjsje Peerdeman did not see the blessed Madonna again for a long time. But strangely enough, as if a spiritual warfare were somehow being waged around her, she was attacked by an invisible "devil" when she was twenty-nine.

Members of the Peerdeman family, as well as their friends and neighbors, bore startled witness to the perverse demonic tactics set against Tjsje. Not only did her physical body receive pinches and pokes from unseen hands, the doors in the household kept banging open and shut and furniture bumped about the room. In addition, an eerie high-pitched whistling sound could be heard, and from time to time a nauseating odor would invade the home without any apparent reason.

At first the pragmatic Peerdeman scoffed when his

neighbors admonished him that such manifestations could only be the result of a visitation from demonic forces, but when Tjsje succumbed to a violent seizure, he decided to call for Father Frehe.

The priest administered the rites of exorcism, and the intensity of the religious ritual successfully accomplished the banishment of his daughter's invisible tormenters.

It was not until eleven years later that Tjsje once again saw her beautiful woman. Tjsje was now a spinster of forty, and the Netherlands was occupied by the army of Nazi Germany.

One evening the Peerdemans invited Father Frehe to share a meal. In the midst of this family gathering and in the presence of the clergyman who had eradicated all records of the beautiful lady's early manifestations, Tjsje beheld her marvelous celestial visitor once again.

As the Peerdemans and their guest sat silently in stunned amazement, Tjsje relayed the date on which the war would end and received dictation for a prayer that the lady wished to have distributed.

"Ask her who she is," Father Frehe demanded.

"You shall call me Woman of All People," the beautiful woman told Tjsje.

From that time onward, Tjsje Peerdeman saw the heavenly visitor again and again, more than fifty times. The Hungarian Revolution of 1956, the numerous wars and skirmishes in the Middle East, and the communist seizure of mainland China were among the numerous global occurrences reported to have been accurately predicted.

Mother Mary told Tjsje that her visitations with her would culminate on Mary's Day, May 31, 1958. To observe and honor the occasion, Roman Catholics from all over the world made pilgrimages to Amsterdam, and they returned with reports of fulfilled prayers and miracle healings.

After the 1958 visitation Tjsje commissioned a German painter, Heinrich Repke, to prepare a portrait of the Woman of All People. Following her description to the last brush stroke, Repke achieved a portrait that has been reproduced and distributed throughout the world. The inspired picture portrays the Blessed Mother as a lovely woman with dark curls, dressed in a flowing white gown and standing on a globe.

The messages which the Blessed Mother dictated to Tjsje Peerdeman were written down in a book that contains prophecies of political strife, a concrete method of achieving deliverance, and a demand that Mary shall be confirmed as co-savior, mediatrix, and intercessor in a new religious dogma. Future predictions tell of a dramatic political division of Europe and warn of a ghastly secret weapon that may be unleashed on mankind.

Leading Humankind Back to the God Light Within

While meditating on April 18, 1995, Lori Jean Flory of Conifer, Colorado, was shown a vision from the "light essence" of Mother Mary.

"She was dressed in a beautiful blue dress and wore a veil of blue light. Her arms were outstretched as though her body was forming a cross. On both of her arms, little birds sat chirping and singing."

Lori Jean is internationally known as one who regularly receives inspired communications from the angels. Together with her husband, Charles, Lori Jean distributes the "Enchanted Spirits" newsletter through her Touch of Wings publishing company. She is also the author of *The Wisdom Teachings of Archangel Michael*, a compilation of loving messages from the Prince of the Heavenly Hosts that she received in a series of contact sessions from October 1993 to April 1995.

Shortly after Archangel Michael had completed his transmissions to Lori Jean, she began to receive dictations from Jesus, Mother Mary, and the angels. The following is an excerpt from a work in progress.

April 11, 1995 (9:53 A.M.) from Mother Mary:

"Sweet Children of the Earth, I come forth with the love, the reverence, the faith and respect of a mother to wrap my arms in love completely around the Earth and around each one of you. Beloved children, I come to lead you back to the God light that lives within the heart and shines through the eyes when love is expressed. Words are not necessary to express love from the heart or the eyes.

"I seek to reconnect your knowing that *all* are interconnected. The traditional Native Americans have always known this, and it is time for all peoples to return to the fold of love and respect. It is time to exhibit compassion and acceptance of one another. It is time for all to return once again to the knowing that there is only one light of many names that encompasses only one love for all hearts. Many roads, many beliefs, lead to the same light of God that is *one*.

"It is time for humankind to live in harmony with all birds and animals upon the planet. It is thus time for humankind to become clearer and more aware that there are beings not seen with physical eyes who serve the God force within the subtle ethers. When you develop a sense of innocence and a reverence for all of life, you may become more aware of those who serve within the Angelic Kingdom.

"Is it not said that as one becomes as a child that the Kingdom of Heaven is found within? As one allows oneself to become innocent, the gifts of heaven are bestowed from within and from above.

"Return to love, dear children of Light. Return to that which you have always known is true—that there is a God that loves you.

"Let us wrap our arms around you, and in so doing, wrap your arms in love around each other. In this way Mother Earth will be encompassed in a giant embrace of love.

"Love your Mother Earth, beloved ones. It is she who sustains you upon her surface. She loves you. You are precious to her—for the Earth Mother is a spirit as well as a planetary being."

The Days Approach for the Testing of Souls

Since 1987, Nancy Fowler, a middle-aged farm woman from Conyers, Georgia, has been receiving daily messages from Mother Mary. Then, on the thirteenth of each month, beginning in 1990, apparitions of Mary and Jesus began to appear. By 1993 as many as 50,000 pilgrims could be expected to gather for each month's demonstration of the divine.

Anne Marie Hancock's 1993 book, *Wake Up, America*, quotes Mrs. Fowler's confessor, Fr. Joachim Tierney, as claiming to have witnessed wondrous healings; miracles of the sun, suggestive of Fatima; the transformation of silver rosaries into gold; and the strong scent of roses, indicating the presence of the Immaculate Heart of Mary.

Carol Bradford told Ms. Hancock of seeing the sun ". . . spinning, dancing, and getting brighter." The area in the sky near the sun became "blue, pink, green, yellow, and then became bathed in a gold light."

Mother Mary speaks often to Mrs. Fowler about the necessity of the citizens of America to practice prayer and sacrifice. The Queen of Heaven also admonishes all to "be loving and giving. Do nothing to lose a soul." The days approach, she warns for the testing of souls. "Put God first in your lives . . . keep His laws . . . live simply and humbly. God's mercy will soon change to God's justice."

In recent years Mother Mary has issued many advisory cautions regarding coming cataclysms and Earth changes. To Mrs. Fowler she has stated that the numerous sins of humankind are increasing:

> A sign will be given in the heavens when it will be too late to convert. A great punishment is coming to California. All over the Earth: more hurricanes, tornadoes, violent storms, great tidal waves, earthquakes, and volcanoes. The "new Heaven and new Earth" . . .

are coming, but first the old will be destroyed. Fire will fall from Heaven; the Earth will be plunged in darkness.

Mary's Message Must Be Spread to All of God's Children

Rosa Lopez of Hollywood, Florida, was one of those who made a pilgrimage to the farm in Conyers, Georgia, 1992. A devout Catholic who had fled to Florida from Castro's Cuba with her husband, Jasinto, in 1967, she had been left bedridden after a series of painful surgeries in 1982. Encouraged by the effects of a bottle of holy water taken from the Fowlers' well that had been sent to her by a cousin, Rosa vowed to visit the farm where so many thousands had witnessed apparitions of the Blessed Mother. She returned to Florida, walking proudly, nearly pain-free, the blessed recipient of a healing miracle.

In April 1993, Rosa received yet another miracle. The Son of God manifested to her and proclaimed that she had been chosen to be a messenger for Mother Mary.

Soon the mother of two began receiving messages directly from the Divine Mother, who greeted her as Rosa Lopez now greets the thousands of faithful who visit her modest blue and white house: "I love you and bless you, and all that you bring with you. May you be well, my child. I am your loving mother, the Virgin Mary."

Not long after the first messages began to manifest, Rosa became aware of a shimmering, oval-shaped light that appeared on a statue of Mother Mary that stood outside their home. At the same time the scent of roses would fill the air. Wherever she looked, the strange light would seem to follow her.

Today Rosa ministers daily to the sick, sometimes going without meals to make herself available to those who have come to be blessed.

"My life has changed completely," she has said. "But

this is the world of Mary, and her message must be spread to all of God's children. I am but a small ant in the community of Mother Mary's messengers."

The Power of Mother Mary's Presence

Clarisa Bernhardt of Winnipeg, Manitoba, Canada, is one of North America's best-known psychic sensitives and one of our dearest friends. When we mentioned the topic of our present book project, Clarisa told us that she had been blessed with two visitations from Mother Mary.

In retrospect, it would seem that the first manifestation created a miracle of mother and child reunion for Clarisa and that the second appearance was designed to employ her as a messenger of healing for someone else. We'll share the first of Clarisa's heavenly encounters in this chapter.

In the early 1970s, she had accompanied her late husband, Russ, to Los Gatos, California, where he was performing his popular one-man show, *Scrooge, In Person*, as part of the gala Christmas season at the Olde Town Theatre and Shopping Center. Clarisa remembered Los Gatos as appearing like a giant picture postcard of holiday decorations and good cheer.

On the morning of November 3, she dropped by the theatre where Russ was rehearsing to let him knew that she was doing a special taped interview for her radio show that day, so she might be a bit later than usual.

"I remember that it was fairly early, about eight-thirty a.m.," Clarisa told us. "A gentle, brief morning shower had freshened the pines with a lovely fragrance."

Puzzled to find the front door to the theatre locked, she recalled a stairway that would take her to the bell tower, where she could crawl through a window and enter the theatre.

"When I reached the bell tower, I paused for a

moment to enjoy the gorgeous rainbow that arched over the mountains, then I found my way in. I went through the balcony and down the stairs to the main theatre area.

"As I entered on the right side and crossed behind the last row of seats, I was aware that I was alone in the theatre. Obviously Russ was not rehearsing at this time.

"Reaching the aisle on the left, I started down toward the stage. Then I stopped as if frozen, for there, standing in the area just below the stage, was a beautiful lady in an off-white, eggshell-colored robe with a cowl that covered her hair and accented her lovely face. She was looking directly at me. I could see a beautiful and brilliant light around her. Her countenance was glowing, yet it did not diminish my ability to see her.

"I closed my eyes, quickly blinking them, then opened them again, as if to clear my vision. *But she was still there, still looking directly at me*—but now she was also smiling at me.

"I could feel the power from her eyes as she looked at me. I looked back at her intently, trying calmly to observe as many details as possible. I wanted to etch her in my memory. (And to this day, I can close my eyes and instantly recall that magnificent experience and see her as if it's happening all over again.)"

And then she was gone. Clarisa estimated that the experience had occurred within a time factor of about a minute, but it seemed as though time had been standing still.

"I wish I could have asked her many things," Clarisa admitted, "but I had not attempted to speak. Nor, as I recall, did I feel able to speak. I was completely overwhelmed. I had just seen Mary and been in the presence of the Holy Mother."

Clarisa knew, of course, that the visitation was something important and significant in her life. In the weeks that followed, she was privileged to have numerous mystical experiences and visions.

"But one very special blessing manifested to heal the ache in my heart," Clarisa said. "It was truly an answer to my many prayers. I was reunited with my dear son Stuart, who had been separated from me following tumultuous family events some years before. No matter how desperately I had tried to mend the situation, nothing had worked. The family rift keeping us apart had seemed impossible to change—and then almost instantly and miraculously, we were together again. It was truly a miracle. I will forever be thankful to Mother Mary for accomplishing such an 'impossible' task."

Twenty-four Ways Mother Mary Might Appear to You

In the early 1970s, Reverend B. W. Palmer, a retired Methodist clergyman from Haines City, Florida, wrote to inform us that he had spent many years collecting hundreds of contemporary visions of the Holy Mother. His exhaustive research on the subject, which he kindly shared with us, indicated that there were at least twenty-four methods that Mother Mary utilized to manifest her image to her children on Earth.

1. The skies appear to open up, and Mary appears to descend to Earth with a band of angels.
2. In the presence of a human witness, Mary appears to descend in a shaft of light.
3. Mother Mary appears or disappears through a solid object, such as a door or a wall.
4. Witnesses may hear footsteps outside the house. When they hear a knock at the door, they open it to behold the Holy Mother.
5. The Madonna can also appear as though she is a picture on the wall.
6. Witnesses may awaken because they feel a spiritual presence in the room or they may feel someone's touch. When they open their eyes, they see the Holy Mother bending over them.

7. An angel may first appear to the witnesses and lead them to the materialization of Mother Mary.

8. A witness may see the face of Mary appear above a person who is desperately in need of help.

9. Witnesses may hear a voice that tells them to go to a certain place and to do a certain thing. When they comply, they encounter the Holy Mother.

10. The figure of Mother Mary may appear in the sky greatly magnified.

11. Witnesses may be awakened by what they at first suppose is the light of a very bright moon. In the next few moments they see the Madonna.

12. The Virgin Mary has often been seen appearing out of a cloud and moving toward witnesses. She has also often used clouds to make her departure.

13. A cloud or a heavy mist may materialize in a witness's room. Out of that mist Mother Mary will appear.

14. During the Fatima miracle, the Holy Mother appeared to the three children in exactly the same way. As often as they were interrogated, all three consistently gave the same description of what they had seen. In many cases, however, Mother Mary appears to several witnesses at the same time and is seen in different ways by the individual percipients. To one witness at the scene of the manifestation she may appear as a ball of light; to another, a flash of lightning; to yet another as a disembodied voice.

15. On many occasions Mary appears in a room occupied by several people and yet is seen by only one or two witnesses. The others may see angels or nothing at all.

16. Mother Mary often appears in the dreams of witnesses to her glory. Many times such a manifestation will bring about a healing to the witness.

17. After she has manifested, the Madonna may vanish suddenly, or she may fade away slowly, moving into a cloud or the ceiling, doors, or floors. She may also

walk away from the witnesses, fading from view as she moves farther and farther away from them.

18. In most visions of the Holy Mother, only the witnesses singled out for communications may see or hear her, even though there may be thousands of people present, such as occurred during the Fatima appearances.

19. Mother Mary often manifests in a strange light that illumines both the holy figure and the witnesses. In some of these cases, the light usually appeared first, followed by the manifestation of Mary.

20. In a number of visionary experiences, the witnesses said that they did not see the Holy Mother, but they were aware of her presence through the manifestation of a supernatural light or through a voice that came to them.

21. Numerous men and women have experienced out-of-body phenomena in which they claimed to have seen the Holy Mother looking after them.

22. In other out-of-body experiences, people claimed to have seen Mother Mary together with deceased friends or relatives.

23. In still other out-of-body experiences, people have claimed to have perceived the lower-spirit worlds where good spirits attempt to assist lower-level entities and where Mother Mary and her attending angels seek to give solace and comfort.

24. During near-death experiences, men and women have returned to consciousness stating they journeyed to heaven, where they saw the Holy Mother together with deceased friends or relatives and attending hosts of angels.

CHAPTER 3

We Want a Loving Mother Who Will Speak for Us

Annie Kirkwood, author of the international best-seller *Mary's Message to the World*, is quick to stress that Mother Mary is not the exclusive possession of any one religious group—the Holy Mother's love and her messages are for the world.

Both Annie and her husband, Byron, are from a Methodist background, so when Mary began to manifest to her in 1987, she naively protested that she was not a Catholic. The Blessed Mother quickly assured her that neither was she a member of that earthly denomination. Mary went on to explain that she was currently giving messages to individuals of all faiths, all over the planet.

When we spoke to Annie and Byron Kirkwood in September 1995, they had just completed a move to a new home in Oklahoma. Still surrounded by unpacked boxes, they graciously took time from their settling-in schedule to speak to us about the phenomenal acceptance of their books and the increasingly widespread sightings of Mother Mary throughout the world.

"I realized that not everyone would agree with the contents of *Mary's Message to the World*," Annie said, "but it was what I had received. I just hope that the world will heed the warnings that Mary gives."

In the book Annie wrote: "Those who believe and pray will do so. Those who argue and disagree will never be convinced. Those who believe will believe; and those who will not, will not—and it is as simple as that."

Mother Mary commented: "It is among the common folk that this message will spread, for all nations, all religions, and all people. The government officials are—as always—too caught up in their own importance to give thought to any other kind of life."

From the beginning Annie Kirkwood has been clear that *Mary's Message to the World* was Mother Mary's message, not hers. In her latest book, *Mary's Message of Hope*, she admits that she feels awed that she was selected to bring forth the message:

> It is clear to me that *I am the messenger and not the message*. The words came through me and did not originate in me. I am working hard to put the message into effect. There are no magic potions, just a lot of diligence, work, and effort. . . . But the rewards are magnificent: unconditional love, peace, hope, joy, and a way to feel really connected to your true essence.

Both Byron and Annie told us that their work with Mother Mary has enriched their personal lives. "It has enhanced our marriage, strengthened our love, and brought us closer together than ever," she said.

However, the Kirkwoods do not hestitate to inform others that it is not their function to serve as personal guides and role models.

"We tell people that they need to listen to their inner heart and learn to trust in themselves," Annie said. "If you depend on me for your inner guidance, then you have missed one of the main principles of Mother Mary's message. Your guidepost is within you—not in me or Byron, or anyone else.

"I refuse to be used by anyone for their guidance. To do so would mean I haven't fully understood Mother Mary's call to seek within. It could mean that I have fallen into the erroneous thinking that I, Annie, could save someone."

Annie explained how she had received *Mary's Message to the World* and other words of inspiration from Mary. First, she would sense the house filling with the scent of roses; then she would heed an inner voice that sent her to the computer keyboard to take dictation from Mother Mary.

But had she ever *seen* the Blessed Mother?

In *Mary's Message of Hope* she describes an experience on August 15, 1992, when sixty or more people gathered with her near a lake at sunset:

> About 7:30 P.M., two ladies noticed the sun spinning. Then the sun began to change colors. . . . I was fortunate enough to see Mother Mary as a wisp of white vapor in the shape of a Madonna image on top of a tree limb; then she vanished. Then in the horizon along the setting sun, I saw Her as the standing madonna shape, all teal blue with pink coming out from around her. She also appeared as a large blue ball of light.

We wondered what kind of acceptance *Mary's Message to the World* had received among the more orthodox Christian believers—perhaps, especially, Roman Catholics.

"The reaction has ranged from anger to total acceptance," Annie replied.

What things in the book had most upset the orthodox mind?

"Many orthodox Christians were troubled by the fact that Mary mentioned reincarnation and past lives," Annie answered. "Orthodox Roman Catholics were most upset by Mother Mary stating that she had had several children in addition to Jesus."

Byron added that there had been a great deal of "under the table" support, however. "Several nuns and priests have written us 'unofficial' letters of encouragement."

We speculated that Pope John Paul II's emphasis on

Mother Mary might help to create a more open attitude toward men and women receiving messages from the Holy Mother.

"Only if he becomes more open and accepting of Marian messages from other than those who claim to receive only 'party-line' utterances," Annie said.

"Mary really emphasized to me that she had come to Earth this time as God's agent. She wants everyone to understand that God is beyond gender. Although we think of God as masculine, God is also maternal.

"Mary comes this time not so much as her historical self, but as a nuturing maternal figure. She wants to remind the world that God is also loving as a mother is loving."

Annie has observed how hungry the great masses of people appear to be for a mother-grandmother kind of love. "The world is tired of the angry father God. It now wants a loving mother."

And why, we wanted to know, has Mary decided to come with such power at this time?

"Mary appears now because time is short," Annie told us. "She has come to advise us that humankind is about to take a dramatic evolutionary step forward. But we must prepare for a number of changes in our lives and in our planet."

Mother Mary Issues Warnings of Earth Changes for the "End Time"

Mother Mary's warnings, as received by Annie Kirkwood through "cosmic dictation," include some rather grim future occurrences.

She advises that there are forces at work that are causing the planet to change direction. Our very solar system is altering itself, realigning the planets, as other galaxies also grow, divide, and splinter. Approaching Earth changes and coming catastrophes will move mountains and upturn oceans, thus causing new lands to rise out of the seas and some coastal regions to be inundated and return to the ocean floor. Land and sea animals will die in great numbers, and many wild creatures will become extinct.

There will be appalling increases in earthquakes and volcanoes—many in areas where such violent natural occurrences have never before taken place. Quakes will create havoc in such nations as Italy, Greece, Russia, Turkey, China, Colombia, Japan, and those in the region of the Himalayan Mountains.

Weather patterns will undergo dramatic changes, with winter months colder and wetter in many regions. There will be great storms in the Indies. Polar ice caps will melt, releasing large chunks of ice to endanger ships and seashores, and causing the sea level to rise, thus altering numerous coastlines. A good portion of the West Coast of the United States will disappear, and the East Coast will also undergo severe changes.

Mother Mary also advises that the period from 1996 to 2000 will bring about an increased number of UFO sightings. UFO reports will be filed across the world on an almost daily basis.

We live now in what many have called "the end time." Mother Mary tells us to clear our hearts of malice, fear, and anger. We have the choice to live in God's fear or in God's love. A new era for humankind will occur when all choose to live in peace. Love will be the answer. And with the new renaissance for humankind there will appear a new species of humanity upon Earth.

Prayers to God Can Alleviate the Coming Cataclysms

"I wanted to leave the prophecies about Earth changes out of *Mary's Message to the World*," Annie said. "I didn't want to instill fear into people's hearts. Fear is not to be the main thrust of the book. But Mother Mary told me that time was short, that people must be warned."

Byron explained that they tried their best to inform people how to prepare for the coming Earth changes in his book *Survival Guide for the New Millennium*. "I'm an old Boy Scout, and I've always believed in their motto, 'Be prepared.' I suppose in my aspect of the mission, I've tried to concentrate on helping people to prepare physically, mentally, and emotionally."

Annie needed to explain further the inclusion of some dire predictions in *Mary's Message to the World* and Mother Mary's qualifying teachings. "She wants us to understand that these predictions can be alleviated or lessened with prayer. Again and again Mother Mary tells us to 'pray, pray for the world.' But we must heed the warnings, for she says that the last few years of this century will bring many surprises, many upheavals.

"In spite of this, though, the Earth changes predictions constitute only one-tenth of the book," Annie stressed. "They are not the main focus of the text. The main message is of God's unconditional love for us and Mary's advice that our love can prepare us for any eventuality. We must make peace with ourselves, our future, our God—and then fear will not be a part of our lives.

"We must also remember that God has given us free will and freedom of choice. And through such things as prayer we can change the future to some degree."

In *Mary's Message of Hope*, Annie explains why certain earlier predictions of approaching catastrophes had not occurred on schedule:

> Mother Mary said that because people around the world were, and had been, praying for improvement, the predictions had been delayed six months to one year. . . . I would like to think that we have delayed all the predictions even more. The reason Mother Mary gave Her prophecy was to make us aware that we need to make changes in our hearts and minds today. She wants us to be in continual prayer, to be honest with ourselves, and not to delude ourselves into

thinking that we are helpless. We can foster great changes, but they will come as we foster the changes in our hearts and in our way of thinking.

Mother Mary has informed Annie that each person's truth can come only through that individual: "Let the Father guide you . . . to work through you. Your truth can come only through you. The truth, as it applies to your life and the circumstances in your life, can only come through you.

"As the representative of the divine maternal energy, I am available to all people. I will come to you with angels and with the love of God. Let your prayers be to God, but I am ever ready to help you connect to the Father."

CHAPTER 4

To God's Children of the World

Beverly Hale Watson of Charlotte, North Carolina, has built a solid reputation as a poet and a spiritual teacher. When we contacted her in September 1995, she was already hard at work for the Salvation Army as their Christmas Bureau project director.

Beverly told us that she had been given personal insights from Mother Mary on numerous occasions over the past eight years, and she went on to detail an extraordinary occurrence that had recently transformed a painting she had commissioned for one of her new books.

"Cynthia Seymour-Hyder, who works with me on my books, did a watercolor painting of a dove for me," she said. "After completing the picture, she filled the bathtub with water and dipped the painting into the water. Upon removing the painting, she noticed that there were numerous other items within the artwork that were not found in the original painting.

"After a period of time, the Holy Spirit informed the two of us that the picture told the story of Jesus Christ. In the upper right corner there is a picture of Mary standing face to face with the angel Gabriel. Christ's head is tilted downward with the crown of thorns in the upper left corner. There are red streaks running from this position on the painting to the bottom, which represents the blood He shed for us. The red line going across the bottom of the lower part of the painting represents Earth. You can see the apostles and four rows of people below the tail feathers of the dove. There are children on the very bottom of the picture facing one another. The tail feathers are actually angels in full form . . . the eternal flame can be seen in the middle of the wings. None of these elements were in the original artwork!"

To God's Children of the World— A Message from Mary Given to Beverly Hale Watson

Received September 14, 1995

The time has come for humankind to prepare for the second coming of the Christed One. A "Christed One" is a designation bestowed upon an individual whose soul has reached a certain level of wisdom and knowledge. Christed Ones have served the heavenly Father in many capacities, not only helping others to evolve on Earth, but also those who reside in the "many mansions" that God has prepared for His children in the heavenly realms.

Is it not written, "There are many in My flock of which you know not"?

This is very true, for there is life on many planets who also worship the Creator of all. Some of these "beings" have been known to visit Earth. Those who have been given the eyes to see can validate for the unbeliever that there is far more to God's Kingdom than most people are willing to accept as truth.

Has God not promised every one of you that you can have Heaven on Earth?

It is unfortunate that many of you scoff at this idea without really taking the time to understand that when your personal house is in total order, there is peace inside. Where there is peace, there is contentment. Where there is contentment/peace, there is no fear. Where there is no fear, one truly knows how to live in the flow of life. A house united has great power and strength.

Did not Jesus tell his disciples that his Father would send a counselor, the Spirit of Truth, who would testify about him? (John 15:20)

It is written thus: "When he—the Spirit of Truth— comes, he will guide you into all truth. He will not speak on his own; he will speak only what he hears, and he will tell you what is yet to come." (John 16:13)

Oh, ye of little faith, why do you doubt? Is not God your Father? Is He not capable of helping His children to total perfection?

But you say, "How can I know what I am to do if I cannot hear His voice?"

I say to you, God has *never* quit communicating with His children. It is you who have ceased communicating with Him!

Everyone is so busy "doing things" that there is too little time set aside for just listening to the Master's call.

From the time you were born, He has been communicating with you in thoughts, ideas, dreams, visions, and intuitions. Yet day after day, far too many humans stumble around, never giving a second thought as to just where it is that all of their thoughts and ideas originate.

God has *always* provided Enlightened Ones for each generation so that His messages may be kept *alive*.

Humankind has never been without gifted teachers who were sent to bring forth truth. For eons He has shown people the power of communicating with Him by the example of sages, seers, prophets. All those who possess gifts of the Holy Spirit prove that He *lives within* them and that He can live within *you*! Those who commit themselves unto the Lord shall experience these gifts.

Ask and ye shall receive! Look around you and see individuals who work with the healing touch, while others speak in tongues or serve as interpreters. There are those who see visions through their inner eyes. There are prophets who can foretell the future.

I, Mary, say to you: "In your silence, He can be heard. Listen with all your heart, and eventually you *will* hear from He who resides within."

You ask how I felt when I was told by Gabriel that I was to be the mother of a Christed One?

As a young woman I was totally in disbelief of that which I was told by Gabriel. While I had been reared in a religious community, in my heart I always knew that there was so much more to God's kingdom than I heard presented. I believed in the power of God, and through Him I knew that *all* things were possible.

Inwardly I truly felt as though God was my real Father, and there were many times when I would go alone to the hillsides to pray—and I felt that the two of us communicated together. He would tell me that I was special to Him, but I certainly had no idea that He would decide to bless me as the Mother of His Son.

People of today must also understand that when I resided on Earth, I was no different from any other person when it came to doing the normal things necessary for survival. Joseph and I were average people who had responsibilities and who went through the struggles in our journey through life. We came to Earth, like you, to experience the things that this planet has to offer its residents.

The greatest of these was *love*. It was the most important thing that Jesus taught and spoke about. *Love one another*. For where there is love, there is peace. That is truth!

You ask if I had the gifts of the Holy Spirit and if I worked with them?

Yes, I was so blessed. For hundreds of years before my birth there had been those who had the ability to communicate with angels and messengers of God. However, it was no different in my time, as it is not in yours. The knowledge of these capabilities was not known by the masses or accepted by them. Those who were the students of the higher teachings often removed themselves from public life, for many of them were constantly ridiculed for their knowingness.

Jesus was sent to educate the masses. He was the instrument through which God could show people His power. Jesus was the way-shower. He was sent to validate God's messages and truths.

He was also to prove to humankind that the human soul lives forever. When He returned after His death on the cross so that others might see Him, He proved that one does not die!

It is truth when it is written that I, Mary, did not always understand my Son. He was different from other children in so many ways. He just seemed to "know things" without needing a formal education. He was wise beyond His years, yet He never really talked down to people. Instead He always tried to educate them.

Jesus spoke often in parables, and He told many tales in order to get people to think rather than just giving them a simple answer. He also had a sense of humor, and He truly thirsted to experience all that He could while living on Earth.

I, like so many of His followers, expected Him to establish God's kingdom and power on Earth. I anticipated His removing all those who denied other people the opportunity to know truth and to live in peace. Like so many of His disciples, I wanted those who were obsessed with greed and power at any cost to be reckoned with. Why must there always be fighting and dissension in the world? I hoped that Jesus would remove all elements of discord from the planet.

It was difficult accepting the fact that Jesus had not been sent by His Father for those reasons.

Humankind has always had free will and choice. They make their own decisions. Do they worship worthless idols of a materialistic world—or do they worship the Creator who can provide them with wisdom, knowledge, and inner peace?

God's storehouse of treasures cannot be bought with silver and gold. They are obtained by faith, trust, belief, commitment—and most of all, love of God. Those who will commit themselves to the Heavenly Father shall be richly blessed. The more you give unto others, the more you shall receive.

My Son was a messenger of God, and the two of us continue to bring truth to those who will listen.

We do appear to humans when it is deemed necessary to provide proof to the masses and to certain individuals that there is an eternal existence beyond physical death.

But we are not the only ones who are sent to Earth as teachers. There are many who are also sons and daughters of the Creator who have ministered to many races around the world. They, too, return often to their followers so that God's message may reach the souls of all humankind.

The time has now come when the people of Earth must come to their senses and recognize and stop the negative forces that are controlling the world.

Collectively people must come together and declare their intentions not to tolerate all the crime, corruption, drugs, materialism, false teachings, spiritual untruths, enslavements, and numerous other detrimental things that are taking place and endangering humankind.

People must pull together in love and reach out to one another in order to resolve their differences.

If each person would start in his or her own little corner of the world and begin to spread this concept, eventually peace *would* reign on Earth.

For where there is love, there is God.

Where there is God, there is power and strength.

Where there is love, there is peace within.

When all people understand what it means to have this indescribable peace within their hearts, they will no longer have fear. When the negative forces can no longer create fear within you, they no longer have power over you.

Blessed are those who seek the Lord, for they shall see His Kingdom.

Blessed are those who step out in faith, for they shall know the presence of the Almighty Father.

Surely, if you can see God's hand in everything, you can leave everything in God's hands.

The proof of God's omnipotent power literally surrounds you no matter where you are in this world.

Do not waste your time pursuing materialistic treasures, for they are only temporary possessions for you to hold for a little while. If you seek spiritual enlightenment, you will be able to fulfill the longing of your soul. Therein you shall find your greatest treasure, and it can't be bought with silver or gold.

I, Mary, say to you, "Go in peace and spread God's love around the world. Expect nothing in return, and His blessings shall be returned to you tenfold."

CHAPTER 5

The Wonder and Mystery of Our Lady of Fatima

The astonishing collapse of the Soviet empire in 1991 no doubt came as less of a surprise to those who had faith in the predictions that Mother Mary made to three children outside the Portuguese village of Fatima in 1917. Numerous men and women throughout the world believe that the dissolution of the communist superpower was the work of the Holy Mother and was intended by her to be the fulfillment of a promise that she had made seventy-four years before.

On May 13, 1917, and on the thirteenth day of the following five months, ten-year-old Lucia dos Santos and her cousins, seven-year-old Francisco and nine-year-old Jacinta Marto, were given three prophecies, the first of which forecast the end of World War I (which was still raging at the time of Mary's visitations) and the terrible destruction of an even greater war if humankind failed to repent of its sins.

The second prediction foretold the advent of the Russian Revolution and the subsequent rise of communism, which would "spread its errors throughout the world."

However, Mother Mary promised that if the pope, in concert with all the world's bishops, consecrated Russia to her holy name, the nation would eventually be converted. In 1984, Pope John Paul II consecrated Russia to the Virgin Mary at St. Peter's in Rome. Seven years later, the Soviet Union was shattered.

Lucia kept Mary's third prophecy a secret, but she is said to have entrusted its contents to Pope John XXIII in 1960. The prediction has never been publicly revealed, and it remains the source of much controversy and speculation.

A Mysterious Lady Appears to Three Shepherd Children

When the two bursts of lightning flashed across the sky on that cloudless day of May 13, 1917, the three shepherd children tending the flocks of Antonio dos Santos outside the village of Fatima immediately stopped what they were doing and looked quizzically at one another. Lightning did not come in a clear sky.

In the next few moments the attention of Lucia dos Santos and Francisco and Jacinta Marto was focused on the leaves of an old oak tree in a high plateau that was called Cova da Iria. To their astonishment, they perceived a strange globe of light emanating a kind of iridescent radiance.

The children were frozen with fright as they saw an aura develop in the center of the globe of light.

"There is someone inside the light," Francisco said in a nervous whisper.

"It—it is a woman, a young woman," Jacinta declared.

Later the children would agree that the lovely young woman appeared to be about eighteen years old. As they stared wide-eyed in awe, she told them not to be afraid.

"I will not harm you," she promised.

"Who are you?" the children wanted to know.

"If you return to this very spot on the thirteenth of every month until October, I will tell you then who I am," the mysterious lady said to Lucia, who quickly repeated her words for the other two. (From the very beginning, the Holy Mother spoke only to Lucia.)

"For now," the lady said, "you must keep my appearance a secret. You must tell no one that you have seen me. And you must say your rosary every day!"

And then the ghost, the spirit, whatever it was, vanished almost as suddenly as it had appeared.

The Children Cannot Keep a Secret

Lucia, Jacinta, and Francisco did say their rosary every day, but the lady had asked too much of three children to expect them to remain silent about the wondrous vision that had manifested before them while they tended sheep.

At first Lucia sternly admonished her cousins to keep the spirit's visit a secret, but the experience had inspired so much awe in each of them that she could not be terribly angry when she learned that Jacinta and Francisco had told their parents. It then became easier for her to rationalize the deed when she confessed the incredible event to her own mother and father.

All three of the children received the same reaction from their families. They were scolded for lying.

Francisco could not hold back tears of helplessness when his sister Jacinta held to the story so adamantly that their mother beat her angrily.

Within a few days, the parish priest stopped by their homes and made known his intense displeasure with children who made up silly ghost stories—and then ended up believing them.

He was shocked, he told them. He knew Jacinta to be a devout little girl. Francisco was a quiet, compassionate boy who cared for birds and animals. Lucia, the youngest of seven children—six girls and a boy—was regarded as a religious child who was devoted to the Holy Mother.

How could they, of all the children in the village, tell such foolish stories?

Sixty Witnesses Accompany the Children for the Second Vision

But the story of the mysterious event spread throughout the village, and on June 13 nearly sixty of their neighbors accompanied the three children to the high plateau where the vision had manifested.

Lucia had always been the acknowledged leader of the three. When they arrived at the oak tree, she began to recite her rosary.

Within a few moments she looked to the east and spoke in an excited voice: "I see the lightning. The lady is coming!"

The assembled townsfolk saw no lightning. Nor could even the most willing detect any sign of the mysterious lady. But they could all see the visible signs of ecstatic bliss move over Lucia's features.

"I see something in the leaves of the oak tree," she gasped.

Francisco and Jacinta testified that they, too, could see the lady materializing just as she had a month ago.

Try as they might, the villagers saw nothing. And although they could clearly hear Lucia asking the unseen visitor a number of questions, it was apparent that although Francisco and Jacinta could see the lady, only Lucia could detect her answers.

Although the visitation did not last long, the message of the woman in the oak tree was both sorrowful and startling: Francisco and Jacinta would soon leave their earthly mission and return to Heaven. Lucia would remain on Earth and be responsible for the spreading of the messages of the Immaculate Heart of Mary.

Five Thousand Pilgrims Gather for the Third Vision

From that visionary experience on, Lucia had little trouble disseminating the words of Mary. Although the village of Fatima was populated by only a few hundred inhabitants, the word of the miraculous manifestations of the Holy Mother traveled quickly throughout all of Portugal. By the time July 13 arrived, five thousand pilgrims joined the three children at the foot of the oak tree.

During her third visit, the lady said that World War I would soon end. Since Portugal had been involved in the fierce struggle for more than a year, the gathered crowd could hardly suppress a cheer when Lucia repeated the words of Mother Mary.

There was a proviso, however. "If humanity does not cease offending God, not much time will elapse . . . and another and more terrible war will begin. When there is seen at night illumination by an unknown light, know that this is the great sign which God is giving that He is about to punish the world for its crimes by means of war, famine, persecutions of the church and of the Holy Father."

There was more, but Lucia did not reveal the additional words of Mother Mary until 1927. Because she feared that the Russian Revolution would lead that sprawling nation to become the scourge of God, Mary advised that Russia be consecrated to the Immaculate Heart. If this consecration was effected by the pope and all the bishops, Lucia was assured that, in the end, Christ would be triumphant.

The Children Are Arrested, Threatened to Issue Retractions

After word of the third visitation of the Immaculate Heart had been widely circulated, Lucia, Jacinta, and Francisco were arrested and placed in jail.

At that time the civil authorities were seeking to control and to minimize the influence of the Roman Catholic Church. Although Portugal had always been known as the "Land of Mary," its traditional monarchy had been replaced by a revolutionary republican government. The new regime had already sought to abolish the Catholic sacraments, and they boasted that in two generations they would completely eliminate the Roman Catholic Church in all of Portugal.

And now there were these three peasant children from the hills of Fatima who were about to foment a religious revolution. The only hope the state had was to expose the children as liars—or intimidate them into making full retractions about their supposed visions.

"It's not working," one of the frustrated government interrogators complained to his superior after a few days of attempting to frighten the children into a confession of deceit. "No matter how I growl and snarl at them, they stick by their stories."

At one point the children were shown a large vat of boiling oil. "Confess to me that you made up all these wild stories about a lady in an oak tree, or we're going to throw you into the vat and boil you alive," a brutish officer threatened them.

Even the prospect of being tossed into boiling oil did not deter the three little visionaries from insisting upon the validity of their experiences.

"Don't worry," a smiling government official told the confused interrogators when the threat of boiling oil did not shake the confidence of the children. "We'll soon call their bluff.

"They say that they are to meet with their so-called Immaculate Heart lady on the thirteenth of each month to receive new messages. The day after tomorrow is August 13. Let's see how our little prophets react when their fateful day has arrived—and they are still in jail!"

The sly plan backfired on the jailers.

On August 13, fifteen thousand pilgrims gathered at Cova da Iria. Many had traveled great distances at great personal sacrifice. When they learned that the three young visionaries had been placed in jail, they were outraged.

"How could the authorities do such a terrible thing to such devout children?" the assembled thousands wanted to know. "How could two little girls and a boy be put in jail for having witnessed a holy occurrence?"

The authorities soon discovered that they had stirred up more unrest among the population than they had estimated. A staggering number of people believed in the visions that the children reported. A decision was quickly made to release Lucia, Jacinta, and Francisco before thousands marched on the jail and the police found themselves attempting to quell a riot—or a revolution.

A few days later, the children kept their fourth appointment with the lady—and although they were a bit late, she did appear.

Crowds Beseeching Healing Energy Appear for Fifth Vision

By September 13, the appointed time for the fifth visitation, the children found themselves nearly crushed by the vast crowd that had appeared. Among the pilgrims in the great assemblage were those begging for healing and for the forgiveness of sins. The blind, the crippled, the maimed, the deaf, the terribly ill, they had all come to Fatima to pray for a personal miracle.

In later years Lucia would recall that "all the afflictions of poor humanity were assembled there." Some climbed to the tops of walls and trees to see the children walk by. Others shouted their supplications at Lucia, Francisco, and Jacinta, praying for their intercession with the Holy Mother.

"If these people so humbled themselves before three small and poor children, just because they were mercifully granted the grace to speak to the Mother of God," Lucia writes in her book, *Fatima*, "what would they not do if they saw our Lord Himself in person before them?"

When the three children at last managed to arrive at the oak tree, they began to say the rosary with the people who had clustered around them. After only a little while there appeared the flash of light that prefaced Mother Mary's arrival—and then she manifested before them.

Mary told Lucia that she would heal some of those who had come expecting miraculous cures, but in October she would perform a miracle so that all would believe. She instructed them to continue to say the rosary in order to obtain the cessation of fighting in the war.

"In October," Mother Mary promised, "Our Lord will come, as well as Our Lady of Dolours and Our Lady of Carmel. St. Joseph will appear with the child Jesus to bless the world."

The Church Conducts
Its Investigation of Fatima

It is well known that the Roman Catholic Church has a number of committees and ecclesiastical authorities to examine all matters pertaining to claimed miracles or visitations from holy figures. It is also well known that these same authorities have very exacting standards that most often exhibit a great reserve toward such claims.

How tempting it must have been for the Church to declare the events at Fatima to be a full-blown, authentic visitation of the Holy Mother and deal an effective blow to the smug atheists in the new government who sought to banish Roman Catholicism from all of Portugal. To its credit, the Church resisted such a temptation and sent the Reverend Doctor Manuel Nunes Formigao to investigate the occurrences taking place near the tiny village of Fatima.

Fr. Formigao was immediately struck by certain similarities between the progression of the Fatima visitations with those that had occurred in La Salette, France, in 1846. At that time two shepherd children had seen Mother Mary in a vision and had been told to warn others that great calamities would come to France if its citizenry did not cease offending God.

Lucia admitted that she had heard of the visitation of

Our Lady at La Salette, but she said that the story had never crossed her mind until the priest reminded her of it.

Although Fr. Formigao was impressed with the sincerity of the children, he remained quite uncertain of how much of what they said was simply their own flights of fantasy. He told his superiors that he must wait until the appointed day of October 13 and appraise those events before he could make any kind of objective judgment.

The Day the Sun Danced at Fatima

By early morning on October 13, 1917, all roads to Fatima were clogged with people who had come from all over Portugal and much of Europe to see Mother Mary's promised miracle for themselves. They came hobbling on crutches, carrying their children who were too ill to walk, hoisting others on stretchers. Some had walked all night, the rich and poor alike, all hoping for a cure, a revelation, an absolution. Somehow an estimated seventy thousand people had managed to gather on the Cova da Iria by noon.

A journalist who was present later wrote that nearly all the men and women were barefooted, "the women carrying their footgear in bags on their heads, the men leaning on great staves and carefully grasping umbrellas, also . . . all oblivious to what was going on about them . . . as if lost in a dream, reciting their rosary in a sad, rhythmic chant."

To add to the discomfort, confusion, and impatience of the vast crowd, it began to rain.

Lucia's mother was convinced that it was to be her daughter's last day on Earth, so she insisted on accompanying her to the high plateau outside the village.

At noon, Lucia stood beside her cousins Francisco and Jacinta at the oak tree. It was raining heavily, and the children looked out over a vast sea of umbrellas.

"Close your umbrellas!" Lucia commanded.

As people obeyed her instructions and passed them

along, waves of umbrellas snapped shut, from the nearest rows of pilgrims to those standing hundreds of yards away.

After several minutes of standing unprotected in the downpour, however, the crowd began to get restless—for nothing was happening. It was a chilly day in October. Everyone was soaked, and they were afraid they would all be catching colds or coming down with pneumonia.

Suddenly Lucia cried out that everyone should kneel down. "She is coming!"

Thousands of eyes and ears strained to see and hear what the little ten-year-old girl was perceiving. Try as even the most devout among them endeavored to do, no one could behold Mother Mary other than Lucia and her two cousins.

"What do you want of me?" those nearest the children heard Lucia ask the unseen figure.

Lucia repeated the Lady's words that she wanted a chapel to be built in honor of the Lady of the Rosary. She advised everyone to continue to pray for the early cessation of hostilities so that all the soldiers could return to their homes.

Lucia asked the Lady about the healing of sick persons and the conversion of sinners.

Once again the Lady replied that certain of those who had gathered on the high plateau that day would be healed. But all must amend their lives and ask forgiveness for their sins.

Before Lucia could ask anything more of the Holy Mother, she reported that the Lady suddenly looked very sad and told her to admonish everyone not to continue to offend God, for He was already so much offended.

The rain stopped abruptly, and the clouds parted to allow the sun to appear in a patch of bright blue sky.

Lucia, Jacinta, and Francisco watched the Lady ascend into the sky, and then, alongside the sun, they beheld St. Joseph with the Child Jesus and Our Lady robed in white with a blue mantle.

"St. Joseph and the Christ Jesus have now appeared to bless the world, for they are tracing the sign of the cross with their hands," Lucia reported to all those within the sound of her voice.

"And now we can see Our Lord and Our Lady . . . and I believe it is Our Lady of Dolours."

While no other members of the multitude assembled that day saw the holy figures described by Lucia dos Santos, they beheld a sight equally as astonishing—and perhaps even more incredible. According to thousands of observers, the sun began to spin, extending fiery fingers across the blue sky.

As the sun danced and spun, Earth itself appeared to change colors. At first the terrain seemed cast in a kind of red shadow, which altered color to shades of orange, yellow, green, blue, indigo, and violet.

According to witnesses, this eerie phenomenon repeated itself three times.

Then to the complete horror of the assembled pilgrims, the sun began to plunge toward Earth.

"We could behold the sun shuddering, shaking violently as it began to move closer toward Earth," a journalist commented later.

As if with one voice, thousands of men and women screamed at the terrible sight. Thousands fell to their knees in terror, pleading with God to have mercy. Others knelt silently staring upward, too frightened even to pray. Most of the seventy thousand people who had gathered outside Fatima that day believed that it was the end of the world.

The remarkably dramatic demonstration of supernatural power continued for ten minutes. Finally, as if in answer to the crowd's collective prayer for mercy, the sun ceased its devastating plunge to Earth and began to climb back toward its position in the heavens.

Avelino de Almeida, editor of the newspaper *O Seculo*, had joined the crowd that day as a skeptical journalist who was also very much opposed to the beliefs of the Roman Catholic Church. But on October 13, 1917, he admitted that his cynicism toward religion and his doubts concerning miracles had been severely shaken. Writing in *O Seculo*, he stated:

> Certainly beyond all cosmic laws were the sudden tremblings and movements of the sun, dancing as it were, in typical language of the peasants, before the astonished multitude who gazed in awe. It remains for the competent to pronounce on the dance macabre of the sun, which today at Fatima has made hosannas burst from the breasts of the faithful and naturally has impressed—so witnesses of belief assure me—even freethinkers and other persons not at all interested in religious matters.
>
> To this unbeliever, it was a spectacle unique and incredible if I had not been a witness to it. I can still see the immense crowd turn toward the sun, which reveals itself free of the clouds, and I hear the nearest spectators crying, "Miracle, miracle!"

The Holy Deaths of Francisco and Jacinta

After the day of the dancing sun at Fatima, Lucia, Francisco, and Jacinta were elevated to celebrity status and became the darlings of the secular press. Wherever the children went, crowds gathered to ask them weighty questions about the meaning of life and the world beyond death. Reporters were never far from their sides, and every word that any of the three children uttered was dutifully recorded and published. Photographers declared anywhere the children walked as a golden photo opportunity.

Although Jacinta and Francisco Marto had been told by the Lady that they would die soon, they remained untroubled. In fact, they told anyone who asked about the brief duration of their earthly mission that they were looking forward to returning home to Heaven.

However, Jacinta did become increasingly distressed by

their loss of privacy. She had always been a very sensitive, somewhat intense child, and she was greatly disturbed by what she considered to be the "worship" that the masses directed at them.

As she became increasingly morose and withdrawn, Jacinta began to experience prophetic visions of her own. Most of these glimpses into the future were quite violent and ghastly in nature, and she revealed that she had been shown terrible bombings in France and Holland. London and Frankfurt, she said, would be nearly in ruins as the result of bombs that would rain death from the skies. All these awful things, she foretold, would take place in twenty-five years (i.e., 1942, when the destruction wrought by World War II would be devastating Europe and Great Britain).

Early in 1919, Francisco became ill with influenza, and the children remembered the Lady's prediction that Francisco and Jacinta would not have long to live. On the morning of April 3, the eleven-year-old boy received his first Communion.

That night Lucia visited him and tearfully reminded him not to forget her when he entered the heavenly kingdom. On April 4, at ten o'clock in the morning, he returned to Heaven in the arms of the Holy Mother.

Jacinta became a victim of influenza a few months after her brother's passing. Medical specialists recommended a complicated chest surgery, and she was brought to the Hospital of Dona Stefania in Lisbon.

"The Holy Mother has told me that I will die alone in Lisbon," nine-year-old Jacinta told Lucia before she was transported to the city.

There are many stories concerning the appearances of the Holy Mother to the little girl as Jacinta lay struggling for life in the hospital so far from her village. She repeated a good number of Mary's prophetic visions, and her personal predictions for those around her astounded many.

In one instance, one of the doctors who was treating her asked Jacinta to pray for him before she went to Heaven.

Jacinta sighed and tearfully informed the physician that he and his daughter would enter the heavenly gates before she did.

The startled doctor left Jacinta's room shaking his head in disbelief, but it was not long before he and his daughter were killed in a tragic accident.

On the afternoon of February 20, 1920, the little girl asked a nurse to find a priest so that she could confess her sins and receive the Last Sacraments.

Fr. Periera dos Reis heard her confession, but he explained that he did not have the Holy Eucharist in his immediate possession. He told Jacinta that he would bring it with him the first thing in the morning.

Very calmly, but with authority, Jacinta informed him that morning would be too late. "I am going to die tonight. Please bring me holy Viaticum yet this evening."

Deeply concerned, the priest checked with the doctors at Dona Stefania before he left the hospital that afternoon.

The physicians assured him that Jacinta was in no danger. If he brought the Holy Eucharist in the morning, she would be there to receive it.

Jacinta knew better. At 10:30 P.M., the little girl's condition worsened. Her attending nurse left her bedside to find a doctor. When she returned with him, they found Jacinta Marto dead, a beatific smile upon her lips, as if welcoming the Lady who had come to take her home.

It was as the Holy Mother had told her: She would die alone in Lisbon.

Shortly after the deaths of Jacinta and Francisco Marto, Lucia dos Santos entered a convent school and took the name of Sister Maria das Dores, "Sister Mary of Sorrows." The young woman proved that she had taken seriously the Holy Mother's assignment to spend her life perpetuating the message, the mystery, and the wonder of Fatima.

CHAPTER 6

Mary's Special Mission to Consecrate Russia

Although Mother Mary revealed her request that Russia be consecrated to the Immaculate Heart during her third visit to the children on July 13, 1917, Lucia dos Santos was guided to keep the Lady's desire a secret until 1927. By then she had become a novice in the convent of the Sisters of St. Dorothy in Tuy, Spain, and had experienced two visions of Jesus, who confirmed his mother's request concerning special devotions and gave his divine consent that she reveal the threat from Russia to her confessors at the convent.

Our Lord also gave Lucia permission to reveal certain additional details about the series of 1917 miracles, but He admonished her not to reveal the contents of the third prophecy until 1960.

On June 13, 1929, as she attended chapel in the convent at Tuy, Lucia had a vision of the Most Holy Trinity. Drops of blood were falling from the face of the crucified Jesus, joining with the blood from His wounded side, and flowing into a chalice.

Beneath the right arm of the cross was Our Lady—and in her left hand was her Immaculate Heart. Under the left arm of the cross were large letters that formed the words GRACE AND MERCY.

It was a month short of twelve years since Our Lady had given eleven-year-old Lucia dos Santos the secret about Russia. Now, the young novitiate knew, the moment had come in which the Blessed Mother wished her to make known to the Holy Church her desire for the consecration of Russia and her promise to convert it. It was time to let the holy father know that he, in union with all the bishops of the world, must make the consecration of Russia to Our Lady's Immaculate Heart, thus promising to save it by such means.

Mother Mary instructed Lucia to pray unceasingly and to sacrifice herself in order to achieve her mission of seeing that Russia was consecrated to the Immaculate Heart.

Later, in a sacred communication she was saddened to hear from Our Lady that her warnings had gone unheeded. "One day, however," Mother Mary told Lucia, "they will repent and do it but by then it will be late. Russia will have already spread her errors throughout the world, provoking wars and great persecutions of the Church."

According to one Marian scholar, who prefers to be known only as "Father John," Pope Pius XII took the warnings from Lucia dos Santos [now known as Sister Maria] very seriously. "Many learned Church scholars had already accepted Our Lady of Fatima as 'the woman dressed with the sun' referred to in chapter twelve of *Revelation*, the biblical book of the Apocalypse.

"Later, Pius the Twelfth said that the message of Fatima could not be comprehended unless one understood the great atheistic battle which was taking place in Russia circa 1940. Our Lady was calling for a mobilization of all Christians to become involved in the big fight.

"Biblically and theologically, the message of Fatima was an invitation to co-redemption. Mother Mary was asking all Christians to feel responsible—almost guilty—for the souls that were being lost to communism."

Lucia testified that on July 13, 1917, after the essence of the message of Fatima was revealed, Mother Mary had given the three children a glimpse of Hell. Our Lady told

Lucia that she had compassion for the souls of the poor sinners in Hell, because there were only a few who cared about them. Mary accused humanity of doing little for their brothers and sisters who strayed from God.

In order to save more sinners from being corrupted by communism, Our Lady told little Lucia dos Santos that God wanted to establish the consecration of Russia to her Immaculate Heart.

And what was the heart of Mother Mary?

"Our Lady's heart was first revealed when she told the angel, 'Be it unto me according to thy word,' and when she acknowledged to Elizabeth, 'My soul exults in God, my Savior,' " explained Father John. "And, of course, in a very special way under the cross, when she accepted the sacrifice of her only Son.

"On the fiftieth anniversary of Fatima, Pope Paul VI quoted St. Ambrose's prayerful wish that there be the heart of Mary in every Christian. If every Christian would accept God's will and sing the magnificat with Mary and would say yes to bearing one's personal cross, such unselfish giving would bring about the salvation of millions of souls."

In 1946, Lucia repeated Mother Mary's wish to William Thomas Walsh, an American Catholic scholar: "What Our Lady wants is that the pope and all the bishops in the world consecrate Russia to her Immaculate Heart on one special date. If it is not done, the errors of Russia will spread throughout every country in the world."

If the pope failed to accomplish this act of consecration, Walsh asked her, would the entire world be overrun by communism?

Lucia answered quickly in the affirmative.

Lucia had made her first vows in November 1928 and her final profession in 1934. Essentially secluded since 1948, behind the walls of the convent of the Carmelite order at Coimbra, Portugal, Lucia remained devoted to seeking her own spiritual perfection—and, no doubt, praying for a pope with great courage to unite the bishops and consecrate Russia to Our Lady of Fatima.

In 1984, Pope John Paul II, a pontiff who had taken as his personal motto, "Mary, I am all yours," in concert with all the bishops of the world, consecrated Russia to the Virgin Mary. Seven years later, the vast, sprawling Soviet-controlled communist empire had fallen.

"An Unknown Light in the Sky Is a Great Sign That God Shall Punish the World with War"

It was also during that July 13, 1917, visitation near Fatima that Our Lady of the Rosary spoke to Lucia of a mysterious light in the sky that would herald the onset of a great war that would punish the world for its many crimes and sins.

On the night of January 25, 1938, a strange illumination filled the skies over Western Europe with an eerie crimson glow. Some called the lights a bizarre manifestation of the Aurora Borealis, the Northern Lights. But the peculiar—albeit somewhat frightening—light show was seen clearly from Italy to Great Britain.

From the advantage of our perspective in 1996, we might wonder how anyone could have doubted the accuracy of Mother Mary's prediction that a strange light in the sky in 1938 would herald the onset of a great war.

Among the early rumblings of an approaching worldwide conflict in 1938 were such aggressive and hostile acts as the following:

- Japanese troops entered Tsingtao, China, and installed a puppet government in Nanking.
- Hitler appointed himself war minister of Germany, met with Italian dictator Mussolini in Rome, and established pogroms in Germany.
- France called up its reserves and prepared for an invasion when it saw the Nazi war machine become increasingly mobilized.

- Following the heinous example of his German ally, Mussolini enacted anti-Jewish legislation in Italy.
- United States president Franklin D. Roosevelt appealed to Hitler and Mussolini to cease their nascent program of European conquest, then recalled the U.S. ambassador to Germany.

Our Lady had been certainly correct in her prediction that the unknown light in the sky over Europe would cast a grim glow on the dawn of World War II.

Lucia made no further mention of the prophetic lights until 1941, when she wrote to the Bishop of Leiria regarding Mother Mary's sign, "which the astronomers chose to designate as Aurora Borealis." Be that as it may, she said, "God was pleased in this way to make me understand that His justice was ready to let fall the blow on the guilty nations, and in this way to begin to ask with insistence for . . . the consecration of Russia."

Was 1917 a Special Year?

In 1886, a biblical scholar named Dr. Hartley Grattan Guinness developed a kind of obsession about the year 1917 and its significance to world history. Dr. Guinness's special area of interest was the Old Testament and its many prophets and prophetic occurrences. Through a somewhat esoteric method of time measurement, he was convinced that there was some cosmic link between the year 1917 and A.D. 622, the year of Mohammed's Hegira, which is regarded as the advent of the Muslim era.

"There can be no question," Dr. Guinness wrote, "that those who live to see the year 1917 will have reached one of the most important—perhaps *the* most momentous—of those terminal years of crisis."

Once again we have the advantage of time perspective in that we may look backward to see just how important and momentous the year 1917 actually was. A rapid paging through the history books certainly indicates that the year was not without its share of significant events:

- The October Revolution in Russia put an end to the rule of the czar and a beginning of the reign of communism. Lenin was appointed chief commissar; Trotsky, commissar of foreign affairs.
- The United States declared war on Germany, Hungary, and Austria. General Pershing arrived in Paris to head the American forces.
- The British royal family renounced their German names and titles.
- General Allenby took over the British command in Palestine, thereby taking Jerusalem and putting an end to nearly thirteen centuries of Muslim control.
- Great Britain suffered air attacks.
- Pope Benedict XV pleaded for peace.
- The first armored tank battle took place at Cambrai.
- John Fitzgerald Kennedy was born; first Roman Catholic president of the United States.
- Four women were arrested in front of the White House for picketing on behalf of women's suffrage.
- C. G. Jung published *Psychology of the Unconscious.*

Dr. Guinness was correct in foreseeing 1917 as a year filled with a large number of crises, but perhaps in the long view of things, the most significant occurrences of 1917 might well have been the three little shepherd children of the tiny Portuguese village of Fatima who participated in a series of miracles with Mother Mary.

Pray the Rosary in the Age of Mary

"Perhaps Our Lady of Fatima truly initiated the Marian epoch when she appeared with the rosary in her hand and bade the children, 'Pray the rosary!' " Father John said.

"Sometimes non-Catholics ask me, 'Father, just what is the rosary?' Popes have always recommended using the rosary, but I believe that the Holy Spirit has especially prepared those of us now living in this critical age to be totally like Mary. The rosary is nothing but a meditation on the life, suffering, and glorification of Jesus.

"Since no one was as close to Our Lord as Our Lady, Mary prays with us as we say the rosary. Perhaps she herself didn't always understand all the things that Jesus said and did, but she pondered them in her heart—and she grew in love, wisdom, and knowledge.

"In the miracles at Fatima, Our Lady invites us to meditate and to live the mysteries of her Son under her own personal guidance, and thus fulfill the original divine plan of creation."

Why Pray to Mary?

Father David M. Knight, pastor of Sacred Heart Church in Memphis, Tennessee, the author of twenty-nine books, rhetorically asks, "Why Pray to Mary?" in the Fall 1995 issue of the Association of Marian Helpers' *Bulletin*. Explaining that Catholic veneration of Mary is based on her becoming the Mother of God by freely consenting to give flesh to God, Fr. Knight answers the question he posed by stating:

Every time I ask Mary to pray for me, I feel I am joining God in His choice to let the human race have a part in redeeming the world. When I go to God, not directly, but through Mary, I am echoing God's choice to come into the world, not directly, but through a human being.

When I ask Mary to pray *with* me, it also reminds me that I have a part to play. Because God respects human beings, He wants us to have a part in healing the human race. As He used Mary, He also wants to use me.

What Is the Secret of the Third Fatima Prophecy?

Reverend Augustin Fuentes was startled to see how ashen-faced and emaciated Lucia dos Santos appeared when he called upon her on December 26, 1957. She was now Sister Maria das Dores, a Carmelite nun in the convent of St. Theresa of Jesus in Coimbra, Portugal, and as Roman postulator, he had come to speak to her for the cause of the beatification of her cousins Francisco and Jacinta Marto.

The priest was concerned about her health. "Are you ill, my child?"

"My body suffers because my soul suffers," she replied. "Father, I know that the Blessed Mother is very sad, because not enough people respect her messages at Fatima."

The priest shared her concern. "It is the way of the world, Sister. It is difficult for those who love sin to leave their old ways and come to God."

Sister Lucia shook her head. "Father, neither the good nor the bad respect Mother Mary's words at Fatima.

"The good do not because they are satisfied with their way of goodness, of virtue, so they do not feel that it is important to heed the messages of Fatima.

"The bad do not listen because the chastisement of God is not immediately hovering over them, and they proceed on their sinful ways without paying any attention to the messages. But believe me, Father, God is going to chastise the world."

Fr. Fuentes counseled Lucia at some length, and he could not resist asking a few questions about the third prophecy, the secret message, which was not to be revealed for three more years.

Lucia smiled apologetically. "I am sorry, Father, I cannot

go into greater detail about the message at this time. It must remain a secret, for through the will of the Blessed Virgin, it may be made known only to the holy father in Rome and the bishop at Fatima."

Fr. Fuentes said that he understood. He did not mean to pry.

Sister Lucia reached out and touched his hand. "I can tell you this, Father: The Blessed Mother said many times to my cousins Francisco and Jacinta, as well as to me, that many nations would disappear from the face of the Earth, and Russia would be the instrument of chastisement of Heaven for all the world if we did not bring about the conversion of that unhappy nation."

In 1956, Cardinal Roncalli made a beautiful speech to the thousands of pilgrims who had gathered that day at the shrine at Fatima. He advised the assembled masses that he believed that when the mystery of Fatima was completely revealed, it would be found to be of much greater significance than simply the Miracle of the Sun.

In 1960, as his destiny would have it, Cardinal Roncalli was Pope John XXIII—and it was to him that Lucia dos Santos would reveal the third prophecy of Mother Mary.

Throughout the year a large segment of the world's Roman Catholic, Christian, and spiritually minded population waited eagerly for the Vatican to release the contents of the Blessed Mother's secret message to Lucia.

Thirty-six years later, we are still waiting.

We know that the contents of the Madonna's prophecy were sent to Rome. We know that Pope John XXIII did open the message. But when the Vatican decides to share the words of the third prophecy is completely at the pope's discretion.

Throughout the entire year of 1960, Roman Catholic churches, such as St. Patrick's Cathedral in New York City, received thousands of calls inquiring about the contents of the third prophecy of Fatima.

The official silence of the Vatican invited speculation and rumors. One account said that when Pope John XXIII read the prophecy in the presence of a bishop, both men were so shocked that neither was able to speak for several hours.

Yet another rumor had it that the Blessed Mother's prophecy warned of the destruction of the church because the Western world had failed to heed the admonitions concerning penance and devotion.

One story, perhaps encouraged by the communist party in Italy, said that Mother Mary had ordered the Vatican to distribute its wealth to the poor, regardless of their denomination or beliefs.

There are also those who speculate that there really was no third prophecy from the Madonna. What Lucia dos Santos had actually delivered in 1960 was a mere reiteration of the Blessed Mother's warnings for the Western world to do penance, along with yet another admonition for the pope to consecrate Russia to her name—which was accomplished by Pope John Paul II in 1984.

CHAPTER 7

Expand Your Prayers for Peace and Grace

When Brenda Montgomery of Tollhouse, California, recalled her vision of Mother Mary for us in October 1995, she said that her mind was once again filled with wonder as she remembered the blessed event that had taken place on May 1, 1992, at 1:28 A.M.

"There has not been a day that has gone by without some thought or vision of the Holy Mother entering my thoughts," she told us.

Brenda qualified that she was not a Roman Catholic. She was, however, well known as a teacher of metaphysics, and she had earned a reputation as an accomplished healer. In addition to teaching "All-Encompassing Vibrational Energy and Sound Healing," she is also a professional artist and has served as a channel for various Ascended Masters.

Her religious background consisted of "growing up in a simple country Brethren Church and being sent to Baptist Bible school in the summers."

She explained that she always felt that she had "a real core of spirituality," which she honored as being her "safe place," her "real truth."

Brenda told us that the story of her visionary encounter with Mary was not easy to tell "because it renders me fully conscious of her marvelous energy, and in that blessed energy I am pretty much useless—except to hold that energy and accept the love! I'd like to be able just to sit down and listen to her words when she comes in to channel through me and others that need her."

When we asked Brenda Montgomery to share her experience for this book, she decided that giving the following remembrance "just might be the thing that someone else needs to read right now, and that these wonderful experiences that I have had should be told—because others can have them with just a little trust.

"So I write this account for you as an open letter to the public," she declared, "even though it once again raises the fear that I had while this was taking place. Yes, the fear! I thought maybe it was my time to go! I wasn't so sure at the beginning of the experience that I might not already be dead, for I couldn't move."

A Vision Remembered

I was awakened out of a sound sleep by a touch. It was not my husband poking me to stop me from snoring, but it *was* a real, live person touch on my forehead.

It shocked me awake, and I sat up and looked into the darkness. I turned to the right to see the clock—1:28 A.M. Then I lay back down.

The night was cool, and I pulled the sheet up under my chin. I had not yet taken a breath when a great white light filled the room. It was not a mere light-bulb light, but a light that seemed like a million megawatts! So white! I could not see the source, but it was about where the door to the living room was in front of me and a little to the left.

Then I began to see the outline of a small figure that became clearer as my eyes began to adjust to the bright light.

I could see that the figure was that of a woman, and she appeared to be wearing a veil. The very center of the figure from top to bottom was a pale blue. The veil came to her fingertips, and she was holding a single red rose bud.

My mind was going crazy with ideas of who this figure was, because I just could not fathom that the Blessed Mother would come to visit me. *Me!* A non-Catholic! I lay so still and clutched the sheet so hard that my hands began to ache. I could not move. I felt as if I were made of stone.

I cannot tell you all the things that were going through my head—mostly feelings of inadequacy in the face of the Divine Mother. As she stood looking at me from behind the lace veil, I felt fear—and yet I felt completely open to her energy and her love and whatever was to come. My heart was pounding so hard, I thought once that I just might have a heart attack. And I knew that if I awakened my husband, the vision might be all over. So I remained very still and quiet. I just hung on to those sheets under my chin, barely breathed, and just watched.

I stared at the Divine Mother, and I wondered why she had come to me. Then the following words crossed my mind: "Because you will share this information with many."

Oh, my, I thought. She is talking to me. I began to weep.

She next moved her left arm and motioned with her hand for me to look away from her and to observe what appeared to be a large "television screen." I wondered for a moment how that could be, for the entire wall at the end of our bed is composed of sliding, mirrored closet doors. There was no reflection from the bedroom windows that I could see, and there was no moonlight peeping in. The room was completely dark except for the large "television screen." I was beginning to experience such a joyful expectation that my heart was just pounding!

Alarming Scenes of Destruction

Then I saw on the screen picture after picture. They came slowly, giving me enough time to see each one clearly and to put them all in my memory. They were pictures of the future that I do not like to remember. They were alarming scenes of the destruction of cities, of the mountains. Close to where I live in California, I saw trees crashing down, rocks falling and piling up. I saw vast changes in the Earth at some point in time. I viewed land masses shifting. I perceived water disappearing from the rivers and spreading out and soaking into the land. I understood that total changes were coming upon us. I saw no people at this time so that I would see only the landmarks and remember where those places were.

I was so entranced by the vision that I can't tell you how long this particular picture show took place. I remembered in the month of April all the telephone calls asking me what my guides had told me about the predictions of Nostradamus. I told most of my callers that I didn't ask my guides those kinds of questions because I did not wish to be an alarmist or to cause people to worry. I felt that my path was strictly a spiritual one.

I was wrong! It was that I didn't want to know. Did I feel silly? I need to hear and be shown everything that spirit wants me to see and to hear—and report it. I knew then that sharing the Mother's visit was necessary.

After I had been shown many "photograph stills" of Mother Earth in disarray, I was feeling amazement and some real fear. After all, I live in the mountains—and one side of my house is about five feet off the ground. I had a visual image of how my house might look after a swift shaking. One big movement, and I would be going down the hill that drops some fifty feet to the next level.

Mother Mary Tells How to Be Prepared

Following these pictures of the Earth in upheaval, Beloved Mary told me several things that I should do to prepare my household. She showed me images of myself in the grocery store picking up extra cans of food and water, extra food for our pets, toilet paper, matches, powdered milk. I saw myself picking up certain medical supplies. Candles. Extra batteries. Bleach to purify the water! I would not have thought of that.

Then I saw myself filling the pickup with gas—and keeping it filled in case of emergency. I saw Mother Mary showing me how to shore up the propane tank so that it would not roll down the hill and cause an explosion. She continued to show me all kinds of ideas for keeping safe—and surviving.

Blessed Mary continued to talk about the importance of taking care of oneself and one's family in the time of changes that lie ahead. "To be prepared is sensible and necessary," she said. Then she advised me to speak to my children and to tell them to have extra canned goods and other supplies on hand.

Mother Mary Speaks of the Power of Prayer

The next message from Mary was so important that she seemed almost to be weeping when she spoke, for her voice was so urgent, so loving, so beautiful and blessed.

"You must all pray to Christ, my Son, to God the Father," she said: "You must pray for the Earth, the world, the people, the changing times—you must pray for them all.

"You must pray for healing. In prayer all things are possible. Even Mother Earth can be released from the torments of her changes. Enough prayer can change the universe. Prayer can bring rest to those souls who have passed to the Other Side.

"You must pray for all beings—good or bad. This is your duty to God.

"You may pray to me, and I shall guide your prayers to God if you so choose. Set aside a time to pray, as you would for meditation, and *pray!* Prayer must be done regularly—and in the total knowing that when a prayer goes out from you, it is received in the Light and given to God. The angels are there to guide your prayers to Christ, to God. Do not worry that your small prayer may be wasted upon a deaf ear. *Any* prayer lifted to the heavens will reach God.

"Human beings have not fully understood the power that prayer has. You must believe me when I say that *prayer is the most powerful energy in the universe*. It is your love magnified in Light.

"I come through this simple channel [Brenda Montgomery] for she understands the energy that prayer creates. Even though she cannot understand the energy in mere words, her prayers are magnified in Love as are yours if you offer them in pure love. If you are not praying daily, begin to pray now.

"All prayers are heard. Prayer is the perfect healing for any pain, any discomfort. Prayer given in perfect love is positive power unleashed and used.

"Love the Earth with your prayers. Your future on Earth and in Heaven is defined by the amount of love-energy that you release in prayer. These are words of essence that hold truths beyond your understanding. However, in the demands of these days on Earth, you are to take this message and flow with it—and share it with others.

"I love you and pray for you—and it matters not whether or not you are Catholic, but that you are of pure spirituality and love. My love and peace goes out to you now—and I await; Earth awaits; the Christ, my Son, awaits; God our Father awaits. Bless the world with your prayers."—Mother Mary

A Resolution to Expand Prayers to Find Peace and Grace

After the vision had ended, I thought of all the times that I had sent up a short little prayer, hardly even thinking about it. I thought about all the prayers that I had issued before a healing session began. I thought of all the prayers silently given that were asking blessings only for myself. (I had prayed over my sore knee with a great fervor!) From now on, my prayers would be different! They would be expanded to include all—and I will know that my healing work is attended by the All That Is—and my healing prayers will be expanded and blessed. Thank you, Father-Mother God!

Mother Mary also spoke to me of my question of learning again the love of the Avatar Sathya Sai Baba, and since that time I have again learned to meditate with a silent mind with the help of Ananda, a group whose spiritual teacher is Paramahansa Yogananda. I seem to be finding so much from my past that I need, to allow my enlightenment to be complete.

I was "sent" to Santa Barbara to meet a new friend and meditate in a Vedantic temple, where I heard the nuns sing songs that reverberated in my very bones. They proved to be the sounds that I needed to hear for my healing. How blessed I am to be reunited with spirit and blessed with Mother Mary's vision and her message to me and to the world. We are all so blessed and so loved!

I hope that in sharing with you this blessed moment in time with Mother Mary that you will take up the practice of prayer more fervently.

We can all find a time—or several times—daily to send out our prayers. Prayer does not have to take place in a church or a holy place. You can pray at home at your own altar. You can pray in the car driving down the road. You can pray at work. You can pray any place where you can focus your love to Christ, Mary, God, the Universe, or Divine Essence. Until that day when we are taken up at the Ascension, all of our prayers are much needed now for the survival of the Earth.

Mother Mary's message is for us to "go back to prayer." If we are to find peace and grace, it is now that love must be poured out from us to God.

Heal the Earth through your prayers. Heal the sick— and heal your souls with prayer.

* * *

Brenda Montgomery reminded us that her vision of Mother Mary took place in 1992:

"Many things have taken place since then," she said, "and the Beloved Mary still comes through my channel to those who need her words—and I am totally in awe of that!

"The Earth is still in the process of change, and we are learning of so many ways that we can alter the future—most of it through prayer.

"Think about it, my friends. Mary was just a little Jewish girl who was chosen to be the mother of Jesus. She didn't ask for that, but she is now one of the great channels of spiritual truth for the world—and we love her and respect her words.

"I am so glad that she decided to come through me and bless me with her light and love. Ask for her in your own meditations. She is always available to speak to those who believe in the truth."

CHAPTER 8

The Madonna on the Wall

Mrs. Esther Cotter, a middle-aged housewife in a suburb of Detroit, first noticed the strange shadow on her parlor wall in June 1979.

"I had just painted the wall a cream color," she told us, "so the weird shadow stood out quite plainly. I opened and closed window shades, moved furniture around, and clicked the lights off and on in an attempt to discover what could be casting the unusually shaped shadow on my wall."

All her efforts to solve the mystery of the shadow proved to be in vain.

The thing started to get under her skin.

Try as she might, she could not find any piece of furniture in line with any source of light that could possibly produce that particular shape.

To be completely certain, she moved nearly every stick of furniture in the parlor, yet the shadow remained immobile.

"My experiments with the shades and the lights didn't solve anything, either," she explained. "The shadow was visible in both sunlight and electric light."

In desperation Esther Cotter began to trace the outline of the shadow with a piece of green chalk. If her husband, Jack, who was an insurance adjuster, was to come home, she thought to herself, he would definitely think that she had suffered a serious regression to an undisciplined stage of her childhood.

The very idea, she scolded herself. A grown woman standing there scribbling on the wall with a piece of chalk!

But she had to find out what could be causing the shadow, or she would be ready for tranquilizers—or an asylum.

When she had completed her shadow-outlining project, Esther stepped back to get a clearer image of the maddening shape. Her hand flew to her mouth in surprise when she saw that she had traced the outline of a woman.

An eerie sensation began to prick her flesh. She cast nervous eyes about the parlor. There was no woman in the room but herself.

With hands trembling with sudden fear, Esther quickly set about scrubbing away the outline with soapy water and a brush.

She decided to tell her husband nothing of her bizarre experience, but two days later, she once again saw the shadow on the parlor wall.

Was she going daffy?

Their house was very old, and it'd had a well-lived-in look when they bought it three years before. She called the real-estate agent who had sold the place to them, and she made a discreet inquiry about whether or not there had been a mural on the wall at one time.

"After I had thought the mystery through, this had seemed a logical explanation to me," Esther said. "If there had been an old mural on the wall, its outlines could have begun to show through the cream-colored paint that I had recently applied."

But the real-estate agent seemed absolutely certain when he informed her that the wall in question was a new one and had been added only shortly before their tenure. He assured her that there had been nothing on the wall but paint and plaster.

Once again yielding to an uncontrollable impulse, Esther began to fill in the outlines of the shadow with chalk.

"This time there were more details," she said. "The figure was about five feet tall. She had a lovely oval face with a kind of Oriental look to her."

By now Esther was becoming quite unnerved by the situation, and she asked a friend, Irene Davis, to come over to see what was happening on her wall.

"At first I thought that I had made a real mistake asking Irene to come over," Esther recalled. "She sees a lot of those spooky movies, and she started talking about maybe there was a woman buried in the wall or that there was the ghost of a woman haunting our house."

Esther suggested that she make some coffee and see if they couldn't come up with some other explanations, preferably ones that would be less frightening.

Irene nodded in agreement as she took a last appraisal of the outlined shadow before they went into the kitchen. "It's funny that you can't really see her arms or her hands in this outline you made. It's just her body and head."

When the ladies returned from their coffee break, they were astonished to see that the shadow now included an arm and a hand.

"That just sent shivers up and down my spine," Esther said, "because that indicated that there was some kind of intelligence connected with the shadow—an intelligence that had responded to our conversation."

Esther expected Irene to continue her theory of a ghost haunting the place, but she took a very different approach to the manifestation.

"Just calm down, Esther, and take a fresh look at the figure," her friend told her. "The shadow is that of a woman in profile. And now with the hand and arm added, she appears to be praying."

Esther had to agree.

"And with her head kind of tilted back like that," Irene went on, "you can see that she's looking toward the cruci-fix that hangs on the wall above it."

Irene announced decisively that they were finished with simple outlining. She reached for the box of chalk, picked out two pieces, one blue, the other white, and set about rendering a more ambitious shading of the shadow figure.

"When she was finished, it was clear to see that the shadow was that of the Madonna, of Mother Mary," Esther said. "Irene had colored her dress blue and given her a white veil."

Irene told her to leave it on the wall. "It is a very special blessing for you and your house."

"Jack will have a fit! He complained when I asked him to help me paint the wall. Now when he sees this—"

"I don't think he'll complain," Irene said. "After all, he's a fallen-away Catholic. Maybe this sign will bring him back into the fold."

Esther recalled that Irene left at that point, leaving her to contemplate the mystery on the wall. "Was it really some kind of miracle? Some kind of sign from Mother Mary? I just didn't know."

One thing she soon knew for certain: Irene had not gone silently to her home.

"She must have made a dozen stops, telling people about the Madonna on the Cotters' wall. By the time Jack got home, there were still seven or eight people praying or saying the rosary in our parlor."

Since his dinner was not delayed and the people were quiet and respectful, Jack accepted the peculiar circumstances with much greater grace and goodwill than Esther had expected. In fact, he seemed genuinely intrigued by the whole thing.

"We left the Madonna on our wall for six months, until after Christmas that year," Esther said. "In that time we probably had over three hundred people stop by the house and ask to see the Madonna. We even had three or four folks who claimed a miracle cure. Perhaps most important on a personal note, Jack started going regularly to Mass again.

"I have been asked dozens of times why I think the shadow figure of the Madonna appeared in our house," Esther said. "I simply have no idea. When we removed the image in December 1979, it never returned. My friend Irene says that you should never try to figure out how or why a miracle occurs. Just accept it. I guess I'll just have to leave it at that."

How to Define a Miracle

According to a 1988 Gallup poll, eighty-eight percent of the people in the United States believe in miracles.

"There are always going to be some people who see immediately the hand of God in every coincidence, and those who are going to be skeptical of everything," said Father James Wiseman, associate professor of theology at Catholic University. "And there is a great in-between."

Jon Butler, a Yale University professor of American history who specializes in American religion, defined miracles as physical events that defy the laws of nature: "Most miracles have some physical manifestation that is evident not only to the individuals involved, but may be evident to the people around them. The catch is, how do you explain it?"

CHAPTER 9

A Rosary Manifests for a Circle of Six Women

Nancy Waldron of Lake Forest, Illinois, a member of the Spiritual Advisory Council (SAC), told us of a remarkable group-shared experience with a rosary that materialized from a woman's visionary encounter with the Divine Mother.

"The tale that I am about to relate involves, to my current knowledge, six women," Nancy prefaced her account. "Five of whom are spiritual healers—four trained, one a 'natural.' Four of the women are members of the Spiritual Advisory Council, with the fifth having attended at least one of the SAC's healing services during its annual summer conferences in Lake Forest."

Four of the women, including Nancy, were willing to have this story published. The fifth woman will be referred to as "Rainbow Child."

Nancy stated frankly that she had no information regarding the background of the sixth woman, who set the circle in motion, "other than to know that she claimed to be psychic and that she felt herself to be strongly connected to the Divine Mother's energy."

Although Nancy told us that she did have the woman's name, she did not have her permission to use it, and had "no idea how to get in touch with her" at the present time.

For the purpose of this story, she suggested, "let's just refer to her as 'The Dreamer.'

"While her story is quite startling, to say the least," Nancy said, "there would have been no point in her making it up. And it is also quite interesting and telling that, as you will shortly read, she was able to select the one person out of a crowd, engaged in an ordinary, everyday activity, who is quite talented and experienced in the metaphysical field."

On the morning of October 9, 1988, when Nancy Waldron's account begins, the Chicago area was overcast and gloomy.

Cynthia Felleisen set out for suburban Grayslake Fairgrounds, where a flea market was to be held. She was to fill in for a friend who had expected to sell some products there, but due to a conflict of appointments could not do so.

At midday, a woman—The Dreamer—approached Cynthia at her table and introduced herself, saying that she had something to give to her. She said that the story that went with the object would sound outright crazy, but she swore that it was the truth.

The Dreamer said that she had been waiting since October 30, 1983, for this moment.

She told Cynthia that she had experienced a vivid dream in which the Holy Mother appeared and gave her three rosaries. The Dreamer was to keep one of them for herself. Another was to be given only to the person who would have an auric field that would match the one that she was about to see in the dream. After she had viewed the identifying aura, the dream ended. [It must be mentioned at this point that Cynthia does not remember what was to have happened to the third rosary.]

In the morning when The Dreamer awakened, she sleepily recalled the dream—and then must have been filled with wonder as she came fully awake with three rosaries clutched in her hand.

She immediately got out of bed and wrote down the exact sequence of colors in the aura of the future recipient of the second rosary so she would not forget them.

For five years The Dreamer had carried the rosary from the Divine Mother and the auric description of the recipient wherever she went.

She told Cynthia that she had studied her from a distance for quite some time to be certain that her aura matched exactly the description that Mother had given her.

The Dreamer was positive that Cynthia Felleisen should receive the rosary that had manifested directly from the Divine Mother.

When Cynthia returned home that afternoon, she called Nancy Waldron.

"Cynthia was less than thrilled," Nancy recalled, "because she had been told a number of times that this present lifetime was one wherein she was trying to get over past-life programming as a nun.

"She was all set to get rid of the rosary, but I told her to hang on to it. The Dreamer had waited so long to carry out the part that had been assigned to her by the Divine Mother—and also I felt that she would get a message regarding the rosary somewhere down the line."

At the beginning of the new year, Cynthia received a message during meditation that the energy of the rosary was to be shared.

Later that month, Cynthia brought it to Lake Forest, where Nancy Waldron and Jackie Jackman live. The three friends meditated together from time to time.

"When we took the rosary out of the satin pouch that Cynthia carried it in, it just glowed," Nancy recalled. "And the energy emanating from it was incredible—like touching a live wire!"

The three women were sitting in Jackie's kitchen, which had late-afternoon light, so they decided to take the rosary into a connecting bathroom that did not have a window.

"As Jackie and I held it up between us, I remember the cross shining," Nancy said. "But later on, when Jackie's daughter came home from school and we went to show her the rosary, it did not glow at all.

"The rosary had been out on a table in a light room, so

obviously the common explanation that it glowed because it was made of some kind of phosphorescent material did not hold. The rosary had given off a bright light after being kept in a dark pouch, but it had given off no glow after being left out in a lighted room. According to physics, isn't that the reverse of what usually happens?"

At this point in her account, Nancy Waldron injected a personal note:

"I'm amused that the word *phosphor*, when used poetically, refers to the morning star, or more particularly to Venus. As I'm certain you're aware, those names are also used to refer to the Holy Mother."

On March 3, 1989, Cynthia Felleisen received the message that the rosary was now to be given to Nancy.

"All along I had been very interested in the fact that while the rosary appeared to be nothing more than plain plastic, it was beautifully made with very fine detail," Nancy said. "I brought the rosary to a local jewelry store to speak with the owner, who had established quite a reputation as one knowledgeable in antique pieces and religious icons.

"I told him that allegedly the rosary had been apported [materialized through paranormal or supernatural means]—at which information his eyebrows went shooting up—but he made no comment.

"He went on to study the rosary very carefully, and he said that it was indeed plain plastic, but that it had been made from molds developed in Europe.

"Specifically," he continued, "like fine Bohemian crystal, it was produced from a mold made in Czechoslovakia, which accounts for the piece being a lovely finished product.

"And furthermore," he went on to say, "one can find similar rosaries for sale in only two places in the world—the Vatican in Rome and in Jerusalem."

At first, Nancy said, she kept the rosary on her writing desk. Then she began to carry it with her in her purse, encased in the silk pouch.

Once when she was visiting a holistic healer with an

Association for Research and Enlightenment background, she thought to show him the rosary. He tried to "tune in" to the object, but immediately said that it had totally different energy from anything he had felt before.

Nancy had a number of other subjective experiences with the rosary, such as a meditation in which the Black Madonna appeared.

"I have never been religiously inclined," she said. "I've always believed firmly in a living presence—a universal force underlying everything here on Earth—which, due to my Protestant background, I'm quite comfortable referring to as God. So I'm really perplexed how I got involved with the rosary. But I did."

On February 16, 1990, Jackie and Nancy went to breakfast in Wilmette and then went on to the Bahai temple to meditate.

"During my meditation," Nancy said, "I heard very clearly the words, 'Listen and listen well.'

"When I came out of meditation, I wondered what it was that I was supposed to listen to.

"Then, as I was reaching in my purse for pen and paper in order to write down those words, as well as other things I had visualized, my eye caught the rosary's silk pouch. At that moment I 'got' the words, *Give it to her.*

"Promptly I gave the rosary to Jackie, who burst into tears, since she was so happy to have it. Here it was my birthday breakfast, and I was giving away my prized possession. Oh, well."

Jackie had the rosary from the Divine Mother until August 22, 1990, when she was told during a healing session to give it to Rainbow Child, on whom she was working at the time.

On January 19, 1991, Nancy heard that the rosary had been passed on to Rev. Mary Stewart Walczak.

Then, on January 25, Mary received the message to give it back to Rainbow Child, which she did on February 3, 1991.

"Rainbow Child told me that when it was returned to

her, she heard the words, 'The circle is now complete,' "
Nancy said. "The last few dates may not be exact, as I was
getting the information secondhand at that point, but the
general pattern is correct."

On the last Sunday in April 1992, Nancy Waldron told
us, concluding her interesting account of what she has
humorously labeled the "Roamin' Rosary," the five women
managed to clear their calendars to get together to make
the trip to Holy Hill in Hartland-Wales, Wisconsin.

"Holy Hill is a Catholic church and retreat center run
by Franciscans, which also contains a healing shrine to
which people flock all year 'round. And naturally, as fate
would have it, we arrived there just in time for the healing
service that was to be held that afternoon. I believe they
have a healing service only once or twice a month."

CHAPTER 10

Anchor the Love of God Within You

A young woman from South Carolina, who prefers to be known only as Liberty, told us that she had received "pages and pages" of messages from Mother Mary, but when she learned of our project concerning the global manifestations of Mary, she said that the Mother informed her that she would dictate new messages specifically for this book.

"Mother has been coming through a lot, asking for time at the computer," Liberty explained. "I am in the middle of a very large project that I have been working on for two years, yet I feel the urgency when Mother requests me to type for her. She really wants you to get this information! I feel the love that she has for both of you, so I really can't complain. To be surrounded by the profound love of someone like Mary is so beautiful—as I am sure you both know."

Liberty told us that she has never been a Christian, nor has she ever belonged to any religious organization. She did, however, see her first Light Being at around the age of three, and she continues to see them to the present day. She has also believed all of her life that "God is love," and that she was born on Earth "to do a job for God."

On the "third-dimensional" plane, she is a housewife with a husband and two young children, a boy and a girl.

Her interaction with Mother Mary began in August 1980, shortly after her father's death.

On August 4 of that year, Liberty's father died suddenly from an accidental fall down a cooling tower at work. He was fifty-six years old.

I had always been a "daddy's girl," and from him I learned never to fear death or God. Both, he taught me, were a natural part of our being.

My father died at approximately 5:30 A.M. EST. At the same time I experienced a dream wherein I was attending a funeral, but I could not see who was in the coffin.

My brother had a dream in which he saw someone carrying our father out of the plant, because he was hurt. My brother called the plant, but Father never answered the page.

My sister was driving home on the New Jersey Turnpike from Long Island, New York, at the same time that our father died. She was, in fact, driving Father's Buick Electra. All of a sudden the headlights and the interior lights went out. She pulled into a highway patrol station and the troopers examined the car, but could find nothing wrong. They wouldn't let her drive the Buick, though, and she had to call a friend for a ride. The next day, after she found out about our father's death, our brother took her back to the car, and every light was in perfect working order.

I believe that Father had some knowledge of his approaching death, and he was quite happy about leaving. He was the happiest corpse you could ever see.

When I returned to our parents' home for the funeral, Father's presence was everywhere. I could hear him in the hall, and we spoke to each other freely. He told me that he was leaving Earth and that he was with the angels and Jesus and Mary. He said that he was happy and was very much loved. He told me that he loved me very much, and someday I would understand more of what was truly in existence in the heavenly realms. This was the true beginning of my quest for knowledge concerning spirit.

After the burial, my brothers and sisters and I were sitting in the den in a state of pure depression and anguish with heavy, heavy hearts. I believe that it was my older brother who first said, "God has touched my heart." One by one, the other two repeated the sentiment—and then I did, too. We all felt profound love and peace enter our hearts and become manifest within us.

It was then that I heard these words: *"Fear not, my child, for I am here. I have never left you, and I never will. You are not alone. I love you."*

I asked who it was who was speaking to me—and the reply was, MOTHER.

I did not question it. I felt great, and after three days without food, I was also hungry. I was really in need of spiritual food, and I was provided with it.

In 1990, I found a lump in my breast. I procrastinated, and months went by before the lump became larger and more painful. A friend felt the lump and convinced me to go to the doctor. I made an appointment for the following Monday.

It was Friday, so I packed up my son and went to visit my mother for the weekend. That night I got into bed and immediately felt hands upon me.

A voice said to me, "We have come to help you."

"Help me with what?" I asked.

"You know why we are here," the voice said. "It is time to begin. You are correct when you say that 'God is love,' and you are one who works for God."

I was wide awake when this happened. You can guess the rest. I was healed. You could literally see my breast moving as they removed [disintegrated] the lump.

I know that Jesus and Mary were among the spirit beings who healed me that night.

Divine Mother Energies

Received by Liberty—August 20, 1995

I am here, Liberty. I know of the request from Brad and Sherry Steiger. You are to receive specific messages for their use in their book. It is no accident that you were informed of this project, and I wish to thank you for allowing yourself to be a vehicle for this purpose.

There is a specific area that I wish to address and that is a somewhat technical explanation of the Divine Mother energies and the use of them—what they will do and how they will do it. Yes, there are individuals who are being used to anchor these feminine energies within others—yet to permit it to be told that it is through someone else that these energies must be anchored would not be of total truth. Anyone can anchor the energies within themselves if their intent is in accordance with Divine Will.

I will say that there are upon this planet many beings that are not, as of now, genetically predisposed to receive the Divine Mother energies. It is here that the facilitators will be used to help set in motion the program of Christ Consciousness—the genetically engineered energies of the Divine Mother, if you will. Many beings *are* predisposed to respond to these energies and need only the conscious thought to set in motion the genetic engineering necessary to return to the Adam Kadmon.*

To anchor these energies one has only to request it. It is not something that is done because of the actions of another. It is done because individuals have recognized their divinity and therefore opened their hearts to receive the

*The Jewish Midrash depicts the primal Adam as an androgynous being, both male and female, as does the *Qablah* in its figure of Adam Kadmon.

Divine Mother energies. Such revelations may come to some as visions of Mary or dreams of Seraphic Angels of female appearance or of pure thought and energy by those individuals of a higher vibration.

Christhood is the goal for humanity, and many have answered the call. The star seed, as some have been called, are awakening—and this is due in part to the anchoring of the Divine Mother energies by the very dedicated Christed Beings among you, in the flesh, so to speak. There are millions on Earth who, consciously or subconsciously, are awakening to these energies. It is not something that requires conscious thought processes. It comes from the heart.

It is actually a rather simple process to anchor the energies within yourself and the area of land mass upon which you exist. You may think of the following as a meditation, if you will.

See yourself as an extension of the ALL.

Now visualize a golden-white beam of pure light energies from the heart of Mother straight to your heart. (You may visualize me in whatever form you wish.) Feel awakening now within you the Mother energies already embedded in your being in accordance to the divine blueprint.

Know that it is so, and it is so.

You are in command of your reality. You create and have co-created with the universe long before your incarnations upon this planet, and many of you have come back due to your dedication to the ALL.

Know this, my dear children: We are one in spirit. My beingness is oftentimes represented in many different ways, for I have endeavored to reach through the heart as many as would listen to me.

I *am* the balance to the male energies. There must be a balance of energies before the final days of Ascension, when the Earth shall ascend to its proper place in the universe.

Anchored deep with the Earth herself is an aspect of the Divine Mother. In an effort to throw off some of the male energies that have disabled many in their quest for spiritual awakening, the aspect of Mother held within has pushed her way toward the surface areas of this planet—and you may see the results in the many Light Communities that have formed, grown, and prospered.

If you look at the past two hundred years of this country called the United States, you will see the results of the energies of the Divine Mother. The old thought patterns are disappearing. No longer is it acceptable to believe that one person is better than another because of the color of the skin. More and more people accept the reality that there is a common goal, a common origin, and a common God for all humans.

Yes, there are many so-called hate groups that still exist, but they do not represent the thoughts of the many. These pockets of disharmony will not be able to withstand for long the loving energies of the Mother-Father God and the love of their fellow human beings.

Consider what I have said. Do you not see the shift in consciousness that is occurring? We certainly do, and I must say that the light of human love for God is shining ever so brightly these days. It makes the angels sing! And the song is so beautiful. Someday you will hear it, too.

There are many of you out there now (who are reading this book) who are hearing this music now. Your higher self is making a conscious connection to the soul that is a part of the shift in consciousness. You are reawakening. No longer will there be a separation of spirit and you. No longer will you ask if you are connected to God, for you will know in your heart that you are.

Keep striving toward the goal of At-One-Ment, and you will achieve.

My love to you always.

Now I have asked the aspect of the Divine Mother known as Mary, Mother of Jesus, to speak.

DIVINE MOTHER

Greetings, dear ones of Earth. I am Mary.

Many of you have seen me in the depths of your beingness, and I come today with a message of hope to all of you.

Please know that I am available to you, and I will never leave you if you need me.

What you need to understand is that you and I are one. If you have a perceived need or have a question, those of us in the heavenly realms will endeavor to answer you. But you must realize that you, too, are divine beings. You also have within you the substance of God. You are able to answer your own questions, but you must have the faith and trust in yourself to understand and believe what you receive.

This is a time when great discernment should be used. False prophets are everywhere. Many are putting forth information that many assume to be truth because it is "channeled." You must still use discernment.

There are many levels of knowingness and many levels of truth. In which category or level it is that you reside is unimportant, as you must stay in your own truth and not someone else's. There is no point in searching for truth if you never look within and find your own. I cannot supply your truth for you, and neither can anyone else.

There is but one ultimate authority in this universe. And you have the God spark within, so why would you go to another being for your truth?

I watch people on Earth scrambling for truth, and they are unable to find it because they resist going within. We here in the heavenly realms are here to assist you—not find your truth for you. You must find it. Your path is between you and God. I do not make such decisions.

If anyone on Earth—be they physical or nonphysical—tells you that he or she has the final word on a spiritual matter, I would advise you to use your discernment. Many times there will be a truth within each statement made, but it may not be *your* truth.

I call forth to each of you: Anchor the love of God within you, and you will automatically anchor the Divine Mother energies within—because you will have achieved balance. When balance is achieved, you will experience peace and love for all. And when you have achieved this,

Ascension will occur as a natural process within your atomic structure.

Due to the scientific mind-set of the last Earth century, many humans try to make the Ascension a complicated science. Of course, there are many "scientific" elements involved, but the most important piece is *you*. And you do not have to understand physics to ascend. You need only love, a proper intention, and a deep faith in your abilities, knowing that the God of ALL has put in place for every one of you the ability to do what needs to be done.

Walk in love, my dear, dear friends. In the coming days many will see, feel, touch, and love the Divine Mother energies of which I am the aspect called Mary. Call upon us at any time, for we love you all so dearly. You are not forgotten, dear ones.

My love,

MARY

Divine Mother on Belief

Received September 11, 1995

The subject today is one of belief—belief in the God self.

Today we hear many "affirmations" issuing forth from Earth. We hear them, yet many times there is not enough belief in self to bring them into manifestation.

You can sit all day and say that you are peace or love or joy or whatever, but it will not come to be if you have no belief in what you are saying. You must have a basis to mount any such statements. And that basis is love of God and therefore of self.

This may seem very simple to some of you, yet there are thousands upon thousands of people on Earth who do not understand the very power that they hold within their beings.

All anyone has to do is to "tap into" the God-given powers of love within them to produce marvelous results.

Too many people get no results—and then get angry at those of us in the heavenly realms for not giving them what they want or need. They are not willing to take responsibility for themselves. They wish God to do everything for them, and they refuse to see that they are there on Earth as an extension of God, a true piece of God. They are at one with God.

You can say that you are at one with God, but you must truly know it in your heart.

Look around you. You will see those who truly know that they are at one with God. They are the ones with no need for affirmations. They have affirmed themselves eons ago. They are no longer separated from the love of God. God resides within their hearts and souls. The gifts of the universe seem to flow to them, so they have no need to affirm.

You ask, "Mother, how can I, too, achieve this?" Look into your heart. Can you say that you are at one with God with power and truth and *love* from the very core of who you are?

I cannot answer this question for you. Only you can. And do not look to other persons for this answer. It is between you and God.

I hear many say, "O Mother, I have done these things you advise over and over—and I still struggle to exist here on Earth."

Then I reply to those who so complain, "Look within your heart. If you still struggle, then somewhere within you there is still a shred of disbelief in your God self."

Do not be unduly saddened if you should find that this is so, for even the most talented and gifted among you are still dealing with this issue.

It is a grand statement to make: I am at one with God. For within this statement comes a great deal of responsibility for your brothers and sisters—not only of the Earth, but elsewhere in God's many mansion worlds.

To be all that you as humans were meant to be is the one goal that should always be on your minds, and it is my task to facilitate heart-centered thoughts to bring about such changes in humanity. It may seem to some like an impossible task, but rest assured, humanity is ready. I cannot express to you how many requests I receive every day for the Divine Mother energies. As I have said before, these feminine energies set up the genetic code changes necessary to proceed into the Higher Realms.

It is like a seed that needs water, sunshine, and soil to grow. If the seed gets too little water, sunshine, or soil, it will not grow. Consider the Divine Mother energies to be the perfect growing medium for human souls—premixed, ready to use, and packaged by God.

The Aspect of the Divine Mother Known as Mary Speaks:

O my children of Light, I come to you this day to bring the good news of my Son and of my Father.

Open your heart to receive—and you shall. Ask for me, and I will be with you. Even if you do not see me, you will feel me.

I have spent much time attempting to soothe the hearts and repair the damage to those spirits who must stay on to continue in their roles of servants to the ALL. It is my duty, so to speak.

Many have seen me. Many have felt me. I love every one of you, just as my Son and my Father do. I serve God by caring for the flock. I am a shepherd for those of poor spirit and heavy heart, just as I care for those of a strong and firm belief in God.

I am the love of God incarnate and the God in action.

In the days ahead, a great many of you will be speaking with me. It is so. There will be a great number of sightings of me.

The purpose of these many sightings is to signal the coming changes, for just as the Divine Mother energies facilitate the genetic changes, I, Mary, signal the finality of the change. Know that you will no longer be separated from All That Is and All That Will Ever Be, for you are one with the Creator of All, and you will know this with every breath you take. No one will ever take this knowledge from you, for you are at one with God.

In closing today, I offer this prayer:

Dear Father/Mother God [however you relate to the Creator], see me here in your presence. Know, dear one, that each day I live to serve your will, for it is only thy will that will prevail. All else will fall by the wayside.

I serve you, dear God, forever. I am the power and the Glory of God. I am the love of God.

Love to the Earth,

MOTHER MARY

Question and Answer Session— September 15, 1995

Mary, providing more information regarding affirmations:
An affirmation is only as good as the intent behind it. Affirmations are good for those who need to bolster themselves with the love of God. An affirmation that is made up of just so many words will have little effect on the desired outcome.

I hear so often, "Dear Mary, please help me financially. Please bring me some money."

I can only say that abundance comes to those who help others. A gift given will be returned tenfold if the gift is given without thought of repayment.

Nada, an aspect of the Divine Mother, explaining more about the coming Earth changes:
Earth as an entity will change, just as she always has. Earth grows and changes just like those who dwell upon her. This process may be difficult for those of Earth to

see at times, yet they must understand that change is inevitable.

Mother Earth must transmute the negativity that has engulfed her before she can evolve into higher dimensions. Remember, there is no room for discord or disharmony in the higher realms of existence.

So Mother Earth will evolve, and her people along with her. It is a natural process, and not one to be feared.

You will be seeing many aspects of the Divine Mother. She comes in all forms, suits all tastes and backgrounds. She comes with love for you all.

Reach out to the heavenly realms. We are here, and we wish to help. It is a time for a good cleansing of spirit. Many concentrate upon the physical, but that is easily cleared when compared to the spiritual clearing that many persons need.

Many are concerned about a time of pain or suffering. And I say this: God has provided a training ground filled with wonderful opportunities. The combinations are almost endless.

You chose your path before you ever came to Earth, and now is the time to live that which you have chosen.

Many of you know that your rewards were never to be here on Earth. And this is true for many—yet rewards are relative to soul progression and what you have earned. There are no free rides—even in Heaven.

The divinity within your very being is part and parcel of the Godhead. Call out to me for help, and I will answer.

Mary, on how the Earth changes might be facilitated:

Treat all who cross your path with love. Send love to all—physical and nonphysical.

Do not worry over details. We are doing our part, too, and so do not forget to send us love as well! We need and want your love more than anything else that you could possibly give us. It is the essence of our very being. Love is what we ask of you.

Seek out the quiet place within to settle yourself and

become one with the All That Is. It is not important to seek technologies, for they have always been given to you when they are needed.

Stop resisting the struggle going on within. Give yourself over to God's will, for it is God's will that will be done on Earth as it is in Heaven. There is no need to struggle. Call upon me.

CHAPTER 11

Healing Miracles of Our Lady of Lourdes

The healing Grotto of Bernadette at Lourdes, France, was constructed on the spot where Bernadette Soubrious conversed with Mother Mary in 1858. Since the time the miracle occurred to the young miller's daughter, pilgrims have journeyed to Lourdes to seek healing and salvation from the waters of the natural spring that appeared in the hillside.

The many miracles at Lourdes are well-documented evidence of supernatural healing achieved through the intercession of Mother Mary and the power of faith and prayer. Consistently, for decades, an average of two hundred thousand people visited the shrine every year. The celebration of the hundredth anniversary of Lourdes brought more than two million persons into the tiny community in southern France. And now, in recent years as we progress into the Age of Mary, annual attendance has risen to over five million.

Although there are thousands upon thousands of cures claimed by men and women who immersed themselves in the cold spring waters of the shrine, the Lourdes Medical Bureau has established certain criteria that must be met before they certify a cure as miraculous:

- The affliction must be a serious disease. If it is not classified as incurable, it must be diagnosed as extremely difficult to cure.
- There must be no improvement in the patient's condition prior to the visit to the Lourdes shrine.
- Medication that may have been used must have been judged ineffective.
- The cure must be totally complete.
- The cure must be unquestionably definitive and free of all doubt.

Thousands of pilgrims have left their crutches and canes at the shrine. Thousands more have been cured of advanced cancers. Here are a few of their miraculous stories.

Healed of a Cancer That Had Spread Despite Many Surgeries

When Rose Martin arrived at Lourdes in 1947, her total weight was a scant seventy pounds. She had undergone surgery for cancer of the uterus in February 1947, and the cancer had continued to spread despite several subsequent operations. Doctors could prescribe only morphine to enable the suffering woman to endure the pain of her affliction.

On July 3, 1947, after three baths in the waters of the shrine, Rose Martin returned to her hotel. Her appetite was suddenly ferocious. The awful pain had disappeared. Several medical complications had vanished.

In 1948, Madame Martin was examined by the medical bureau at Lourdes and declared to be totally free of cancer. In the interim she had gained thirty-four pounds. She had become the very picture of health and vitality.

More than twenty leading French doctors and surgeons confirmed the unusual healing. Annual checkups and physical examinations later revealed that she had remained free of the dreaded disease.

On May 3, 1948, the bishop of Nice acted at the request of the Lourdes Medical Commission and declared Rose Martin's healing to be a miraculous cure.

She Arrived at Lourdes with Only a Few Days to Live

When fifteen-year-old Simone Rams of Antwerp, Belgium, underwent an operation in June 1951 to discover the cause of a painfully swelling left thigh, surgeons judged the bone to be cancerous.

Between then and 1959, Simone's condition worsened. The once healthy young girl became a bedridden invalid as her leg rapidly deteriorated.

In desperation her parents suggested a trip to Lourdes to their family physician.

"I'll agree," he said after some deliberation, "but only if she makes the trip on a stretcher with a nurse and doctor accompanying her. Simone is much too weak to travel without constant medical attention."

When she arrived at Lourdes on May 12, 1959, she was considered a terminal cancer case with only a few days to live. The tumor in her thigh was enormous, and the constant pain had drained her strength. The only nourishment her attending physician had managed to get down her was a cup of tea and a small piece of cake.

After her painful journey it was necessary for the Belgian teenager to rest quietly at a Lourdes inn.

"She must build up her strength before she can be carried to the shrine," her doctor advised the girl's parents.

On the morning of May 18, when she was finally carried to the baths, Simone experienced even greater pain than she had previously endured.

But as she was being lowered into the waters, she felt a sense of health surge through her body. "I knew my troubles were gone forever," she said later.

Her attending physician exclaimed that he was "staggered"

when he discovered that the enormous swelling in his patient's left thigh had vanished.

At his request, Simone rose and took a few steps without too much difficulty. Her long illness had weakened her, but she was walking.

Simone announced that she was hungry, and that afternoon she ate her first full meal in years. The heartiness of her appetite was so great that she consumed a great amount of food during both the afternoon and evening meals.

Simone Rams's cure was permanent, complete, and accepted as a miracle by the Lourdes Medical Board after two years of extensive investigation.

Healed of Cancer by Holy Water Taken from the Grotto

One day in the summer of 1970, when Dr. Robert Wasserman, a Los Angeles surgeon, pulled into the service station that he most often frequented for gas and minor repairs for his car, mechanic Steve Wolniak asked if he would take a look at the open sore on the top of his head.

The doctor obliged by giving the man's sore what medics call a "peek and a shriek." But when he saw the deep, festering wound, Dr. Wasserman's professional concern was immediately activated. The sore, about the size of a quarter, had eaten through the bone and had obviously penetrated the mechanic's brain.

Dr. Wasserman was direct and to the point. He stated that he would need tests to confirm his visual diagnosis, but it seemed obvious to him that Wolniak had cancer. Although he was on his way out of town on his summer vacation, Wasserman gave the mechanic the name of a cancer specialist.

Several weeks later, when the doctor returned to Los Angeles, he learned through others at the service station that Wolniak hadn't gone near the specialist.

Concerned for the man's health, Dr. Wasserman called Wolniak and asked him to come to see him in his office.

"He came in about a week later, and I was astonished to see that the hole in his skull was completely closed," Dr. Wasserman told journalist Anson Heath. "There was absolutely no sign of the cancer. It was gone."

Wolniak told the amazed doctor that he had washed the wound each day with holy water that a close friend had brought back from the famous Our Lady of Lourdes shrine. After a number of applications of the holy water, Wolniak said that he simply woke up one morning and the growth was gone.

"That was twenty years ago," Dr. Wasserman said in September 1990. "I still see Steve Wolniak occasionally, and the man is the picture of health. It may be unscientific to say this, but he is a walking miracle."

Mother Mary Heals an Atheist of His Paralysis

The rolling hills of southern France were vivid with colorful autumn leaves during the first week in October 1954. Anton Cartier, a French communist, sat gingerly beside his wife as she drove their secondhand Peugeot toward the Lourdes shrine.

Cartier was a tall, slender man in his mid-fifties with a vigorous athletic appearance. His hair was rumpled and his open-necked sport shirt was improperly buttoned. This was understandable, because Anton Cartier was paralyzed on his left side. Three years previously, he had fallen from a ladder while painting the eaves of his suburban Paris home.

Scores of specialists and medical doctors had treated the paralysis without success, leaving the once robust man complaining to his wife of feeling "like half a man."

Cartier was a dedicated minor official in the French

Communist party. He had learned to sneer at religion during World War II when he had fought with a communist-led group of underground fighters who harassed the Nazis. The brutality and atrocities that he had witnessed had convinced him that there could be no just or loving God. Party eyebrows had arched with surprise when Cartier had married Marie Bindel, a devout young woman who took her Roman Catholicism very seriously.

As one might imagine, there had been fierce arguments in the Cartier home when Marie first suggested the trip to Lourdes to seek a healing from the Blessed Mother.

"Marie, you surely know that I do not believe in such ridiculous things," Anton had said. "Can you imagine what my friends would say if they were even to hear that you were attempting to force me to accept anything from your superstitious religion?"

Marie snorted in derision. "Your friends are a bunch of atheistic reds. What are any of them doing to help cure you, my husband? Do the spirits of Lenin or Stalin bring healing to their followers?"

Cartier had rolled his eyes in frustration. "It is out of the question. The finest doctors in Paris cannot cure me, so I have accepted the ugly fact that I am doomed to lie like this, bedridden, for the rest of my life. You, too, must accept the reality of my hopeless situation."

Marie shook her head in rejection of the inevitability of her husband's fate. "If you have faith in God, you can be healed. If we travel to the shrine at Lourdes and beseech the Holy Mother, Mary may choose to heal you."

Week after week Marie Cartier implored her husband to make the journey to Lourdes, to become a supplicant, a pilgrim to Our Lady's shrine.

Reluctantly Anton at last consented to make the trip. "At least it will shut you up and allow me some peace," he grumbled.

When the couple arrived at Lourdes, Anton Cartier cynically dismissed the colorful pageantry of the processions as primitive superstitious expressions of desperate hope. His lips curled into a sneer at the hundreds of earnest pilgrims and their attentive devotion to the shrine of Mother Mary.

"Do not laugh, monsieur," admonished a *brancardier* who bore stretchers for the faithful who wished to reach the healing waters of the spring. "I have seen many cures with my own eyes."

"Mass hypnotism," Cartier said with a dismissive laugh.

"The healing power of God and the love of Mother Mary," said the stretcher bearer, moving on to help one of the devout.

Later, when he himself was placed in the chilly spring waters of the shrine, Cartier cast a disbelieving glance at the hopeful pilgrims all around him. A fat woman with the ruddy face of a china doll bathed a shriveled arm in the waters. A young girl with a deformed spine was splashed with the healing waters by a friend. An old man, shaking from a palsied trembling, sought the power of healing from the Blessed Mother.

To his left Cartier suddenly found his attention riveted on a small boy whose legs were bound with stainless steel braces. Two unblinking eyes stared sightlessly from beneath a golden strand of boyish hair.

The blind child slipped in the water and flailed his arms. With the limited movement possible in his right arm, Cartier grabbed the slender body.

"Thank you, monsieur," said the grateful boy in a soft whisper. "Will you now pray to Mother Mary for me? I so wish to see the world that everyone talks about."

Cartier awkwardly searched for a word or two of solace to say to the boy. "Perhaps you will see . . . if you have faith."

"This is my fifth trip," the boy said sadly, "and nothing seems to happen. Please pray for me to Mary so that she might intercede for me and ask her holy Son Jesus to let me see."

A sudden wave of compassion engulfed Anton Cartier. Tears welled in his eyes, and he found himself positioning his hands in prayer. The words seem to come from some mouth other than his own as he heard himself saying, "Oh, Mother Mary! If you really do exist, please grant this child the gift of sight. He deserves to see the world in which he has been placed."

It was several minutes before Cartier found the strength to be able to leave the spring waters. He felt very faint, and his heart was palpitating in a strange fashion. He motioned for Marie to come for him with the *brancardiers*.

As the men were helping him onto a stretcher, Cartier felt a peculiar surge of energy in his paralyzed leg. The next moment he found that it was possible to move his left arm.

An hour later, the astonished and grateful man and his wife knelt at a nearby chapel and gave thanks to Mother Mary for the miraculous cure. Not only had the Communist official been healed, but the miracle had also reaffirmed his childhood faith in Christianity. Anton Cartier tore his party cards to shreds and tossed them to the whim of the autumn wind.

Days later, news of the remarkable cure of Cartier swept throughout France. Quite understandably the healing of the former Communist party official became the subject of a great deal of discussion and debate. Some psychiatrists theorized that Cartier had been suffering repressed feelings of guilt for having rejected the religious practices of his youth. This guilt, they suggested, had brought on the paralysis as a self-induced psychosomatic method of punishment. Later, at Lourdes, his pity for the blind boy and the emotional involvement with the whole business of the Lourdes pageantry had shocked the middle-aged man from his psychosomatic paralysis.

Cartier himself shrugged that such psychiatric analyses might make a "pretty theory," but he disagreed with the learned doctors. "I was a complete skeptic until the very moment of my healing."

Freed of his paralysis, Cartier took a job in a Parisian factory and joined his wife in an active, church-centered life.

The Nobel Prize—Winning Scientist Who Witnessed a Miracle

The nurse walked briskly through the corridors of Sept Douleurs hospital. Her stiffly starched uniform rustled as she approached the two doctors waiting in the physicians' lounge. "You may examine the patient now," she told them.

Dr. Alexis Carrel and his French colleague, Dr. Bromillous, a well-known Bordeaux surgeon, followed the nurse to the examination room.

"The patient's name is Marie Bailly. Her entire immediate family has died of tuberculosis," Dr. Bromillous said. "She has tubercular sores, lesions in her lungs, and she has been afflicted with peritonitis for the past several months. She may die at any moment. However, relatives have demanded that she make the trip to the shrine at Lourdes."

Dr. Carrel examined Marie Bailly's thin white face and was dismayed by its emaciated condition. The young woman's abdomen was twisted into a misshapen lump. Her ears and nails were already coloring into a vivid blueness. Her pulse beat raced at an incredible one hundred fifty beats a minute.

"Your opinion, Dr. Carrel?" Dr. Bromillous asked after they had left the patient.

Dr. Carrel shook his head sadly. "She's doomed."

Such a pronouncement by Dr. Alexis Carrel would have been considered definitive by any group of physicians. Until his death in 1944, he was one of the foremost medical authorities in the world. An American surgeon and an experimental biologist, Carrel won the Nobel prize in 1912 in physiology and medicine for his extensive work in suturing blood vessels and transplanting organs. Working with Charles A. Lindbergh, he invented the mechanical heart. He also developed a method of keeping human tissue and organs alive in nutrient solutions.

There was no question that Dr. Carrel was an eminent medical authority and that his diagnosis of a patient's condition would quite likely be accurate. However, when he pronounced Marie Bailly doomed, he had not taken into account the healing powers of Mother Mary.

As Dr. Carrel and his French colleagues drove to Lourdes to observe the activities at the shrine and the waters, a doctor inquired about the American scientist's personal religious convictions.

"I'm afraid my religious ideas have all been destroyed by my scientific investigations," he replied unhesitatingly. "In the nature of intellectual curiosity, I have accompanied a group of patients to Lourdes, but I am a skeptic among the devout pilgrims. I'm interested in examining the claims of alleged cures, but I give little or no credence to them."

"But what about the records of documented cures that you have been allowed to check?" inquired another of his colleagues.

Dr. Carrel admitted that everyone had been very kind in opening medical records for his examination. "But in my opinion too many of the alleged cures could be the result of a form of hysteria rather than an organic disease. The only thing that would convince me, gentlemen, is the cure of an organic disease, such as a cancer disappearing, a bone regrowth, or some congenital dislocation completely vanishing."

"But, Dr. Carrel," one of the French doctors protested, "you must have found documented records of such cures as those that you have mentioned."

The American surgeon nodded. "Yes, but these cures did not occur in front of my eyes, and I did not examine the patients before and after the alleged healings. I am not demeaning the analyses of other doctors, gentlemen, but I am simply pointing out that I personally cannot accept the reality of such healings."

"And if you should witness for yourself such miracle healings occurring?" posed another of the doctors.

"If I should indeed witness such fantastic phenomena

for myself, then I would toss away all of the scientific theories and hypotheses in the world. And I would gladly do so, for such miracles would reaffirm my belief in a higher power," Dr. Carrel answered.

By the time that Dr. Carrel and his colleagues arrived at the healing shrine at Lourdes, several of the pilgrims had already approached the spring.

Glancing about the crowds, he saw Marie Bailly standing in front of the shrine. Her weariness betrayed her, and the feeble movements she made were those of a dying creature. Although he was well accustomed to illness and death in all of their unpleasant manifestations, the sight of the suffering woman clutched his body like an iron fist.

Suddenly Marie Bailly stiffened as if she had been struck by a powerful force that now surged through her pain-wracked body. The stretcher bearers near her stared incomprehensibly at her, and one of them fell to his knees and crossed himself.

Dr. Carrel and his colleagues watched with astonishment as Marie's face clouded momentarily. Then her paleness was replaced by a rosy hue.

Before the doctors' eyes, her swollen abdomen was transformed from a misshapen lump and flattened to a smooth stomach.

Her pulse calmed, and her respiration appeared to be normal.

"I would like a glass of milk, please," Marie asked feebly.

As she eagerly swallowed the milk, the doctors noted that it was the first food that she had been able to consume in almost a week.

Since Dr. Carrel had witnessed the amazing healing, he did not trust his ability to remain objective without other doctors as witnesses during the reexamination. When he returned to the Sept Douleurs hospital, the shaken scientist requested that three other physicians assist in the examination.

Later, one of the French doctors shrugged and told Dr. Carrel, "We can only verify what you already know."

"Please tell me your conclusion," the American scientist asked them.

"Marie Bailly has been cured."

Dr. Carrel tried to reconstruct the miracle that he had just witnessed and make it fit somehow with the reality that he understood. Only an hour before, the young woman had been dying. He knew this to be a fact, for he himself had examined her thoroughly before she had been taken to the healing waters of Lourdes. She had suffered for years from tuberculosis—an organic disease. Her cure had fulfilled all the criteria that he had insisted must be present to satisfy his cynicism regarding supernatural acts of healing.

Suffused with Mother Mary's magnificent energy, Marie Bailly recovered quickly and returned to her home as a completely cured person. The dank stench of death no longer hung over her. She seemed literally to be reborn after her long illness, and her body appeared to glow with health and vitality.

Just as Marie Bailly was cured of her terminal illness at Lourdes, so did Dr. Alexis Carrel leave his skepticism to be submerged in its healing waters. He was transformed from a rigid scoffer into a devout believer in faith healing.

Mary Appears at Lourdes to Heal Man Paralyzed for Sixteen Years

In 1977, mill worker Jean Salaun of La Loupe, France, was stricken with multiple sclerosis. The disease left him almost completely paralyzed, unable to walk, and nearly as helpless as an infant. He had to have someone help him shave, get dressed, and perform daily hygienic tasks.

Salaun was taken to Lourdes in August 1992, but nothing changed in his condition. Undaunted, in August 1993, he asked his son to take him once again to the healing spring waters.

One morning before he was to be taken to the shrine, Jean Salaun was praying to the Blessed Mother to grant him a healing. Then, to his complete astonishment, in the next moment she appeared to him.

"She had blue eyes and was smiling at me," Salaun said later. "She was very young and beautiful, dressed all in white, but barefoot."

Mary commanded him to stand, but Salaun admitted that he was so frightened to be in the presence of the Blessed Mother that he was "petrified."

Later, after his son had helped him bathe in the waters before the shrine, Salaun was deeply disappointed when nothing happened to alleviate his condition. Perhaps, he reasoned, he had offended Mother Mary by not obeying her command to stand when she appeared before him. He decided to return to La Loupe.

The next day, however, when he was resting, he suddenly felt an icy chill move through his body. Then, in the very next moment, a fiery heat came over him.

It was then that Jean Salaun comprehended that he had been healed. He stood up without assistance and stretched both his arms and his legs to be certain that he had been cured.

He began jumping for joy, crying and hugging his wife. With tears streaming down both of their faces, Salaun and his wife thanked God and the Virgin Mary for his miracle.

Dr. Roger Pilon, chief of the Lourdes International Medical Bureau, which investigates claims of miracle healings reported at the shrine, has agreed that there is "no scientific explanation" for Jean Salaun's healing and has decreed it to be a "true miracle."

Dr. Pilon clarified that Salaun's healing was much more than a remission—which, he acknowledged, could occur, usually over several months. Salaun's recovery had occurred literally overnight. "And that's unheard of."

After sixteen years of almost complete paralysis, Jean Salaun now walks with his wife, carries groceries home, rides his bicycle, and visits the sick to inspire them with hope for their conditions.

Father Joseph Hercouet, who organized Salaun's trips to Lourdes, told journalists that there was no medical explanation for such a miraculous cure. "It's truly extraordinary."

Divine Intercession

Mrs. Josephine Hoare was well aware that she had been suffering from chronic nephritis, a severe kidney disease, for quite some time, but when her doctors gave her only two years to live, she decided that a trip to Lourdes would give her a greater chance to enjoy the future.

When the twenty-eight-year-old housewife from London returned home, she claimed that she had been blessed with a healing miracle from Mother Mary. To silence any doubters, she returned to her physicians to verify the miracle that she was certain had occurred.

While they admitted that the disease had become unexplainably dormant, they were reluctant to acknowledge a full-blown Lourdes miracle. Although Josephine joyfully declared that she was about to begin a new life—and a family—her doctors sternly warned her never to attempt to have a child. According to their scientific worldview and their medical expertise, a condition of pregnancy could very well activate the disease and would almost certainly kill her.

Josephine believed in the miracle that Mother Mary had awarded her, and she soon became pregnant.

On December 30, 1973, mother and child were reportedly doing well.

Once again Josephine Hoare claimed divine intercession. And once again her doctors admitted to be completely confounded.

We All Grow in Holiness by Sharing Mary's Relationship to God

In the Fall 1995 issue of the Association of Marian Helpers' *Bulletin*, executive editor Vinny Flynn explains how we may all grow in holiness by sharing in Mary's immaculate relationship with God:

> Pope John Paul II explains that Mary was "the first to receive God's mercy," and she received it in "a particular and exceptional way, as no other person has" (*Rich in Mercy, 9*). Like us, Mary was redeemed by virtue of Christ's saving sacrifice, but, by a special gift of mercy, she was redeemed in advance . . ."fashioned by the Holy Spirit as a *new creature*" and "adorned from the first instant of her conception with the radiance of an *entirely unique holiness.*" *(Lumen Gentium, 56).*

Finney goes on to suggest what the "entirely unique holiness" of this "new creature" means to the individual members of humankind in regard to their own growth in holiness:

> Mary herself gave us the clue at Lourdes. When Bernadette asked her who she was, she didn't *describe* herself as *immaculately conceived*; she *named* herself as *the* Immaculate Conception. Thus she implies that she is not merely holy, but, by the special in-dwelling of her spouse, the Holy Spirit, *she is holiness itself.*

CHAPTER 12

Mother Mary's Holy, Healing Love

It has been said that there are no atheists in frontline trenches when enemy bullets are flying overhead. If Fabio Gregori of Civitavecchia, Italy, is representative of collision victims, then neither are there any atheists among those who survive head-on automobile crashes.

All of Fabio's family and friends knew that he had become extremely devout since his accident in 1993, and no one was at all surprised when he asked their parish priest for a statue of the Blessed Mother for the grotto that he had constructed in their backyard.

Father Pablo gave him a seventeen-inch replica of a full-size statue of the Madonna that stands in Medjugorje, Bosnia. The priest blessed the lovely statuette with holy water and told Fabio that Mary would be his guardian.

On February 2, 1995, Fabio and his wife, Annamaria, were getting ready to attend church when their five-year-old daughter, Jessica, ran into the house shouting that the Virgin Mary was crying.

Jessica took her father's hands and pulled him out to the statue of Mother Mary that he had placed in a special niche in their grotto.

"Annamaria and I couldn't believe our eyes," Fabio later told reporters. "The statue was crying tears of blood.

We threw ourselves on our knees and prayed. I felt shivers of joy and fear all over my body."

Annamaria and Fabio immediately summoned Father Pablo to witness the miracle.

The priest said that he nearly fainted with emotion when he saw the tears of blood flowing from Mary's eyes.

Then, recovering his emotional balance, Father Pablo set about examining the statue very closely. He touched it, tapped it, turned it upside down. "I shook it and knocked it," he said. "There were no tricks. I was certain that those were real tears. It was a miracle!"

The little statue of Mother Mary wept tears of blood for the next four days. Soon Fabio's backyard garden grotto was overrun by thousands of devout and curious people hoping to see for themselves the miracle that was occurring in their city.

On some days the huge crowd of pilgrims was lined up for three miles in front of Fabio's garden. Many of the faithful soaked handkerchiefs in the blood that issued from the statuette's eyes, and some claimed that they were healed of their afflictions after wiping the holy blood on their bodies.

When word of the backyard miracle of Fabio Gregori reached Bishop Girolamo Grillo, he asked that the statue of Mary be turned over to the church for a scientific examination. Fabio willingly complied with the official request.

The scientific commission assembled by Bishop Grillo conducted an extensive examination of the statue, including X rays and a CAT scan.

Bishop Grillo freely admitted his skepticism about the tears of blood issuing from the statuette of the Blessed Mother, but when the commission found no evidence of trickery and ascertained that the tears were composed of human blood, he conceded that he had changed his mind.

As of July 1995, the church was hoping to gather enough evidence to pronounce the event a miracle. But Father Pablo quite likely speaks for the thousands who flocked to Fabio Gregori's garden to witness for themselves what seemed without question to be a miraculous event: "Perhaps Mary wanted to show her deep sorrow for recent outbreaks of crime in this city. Or maybe it was a sign of benevolence toward Fabio, a man who discovered his profound faith after surviving a serious car crash."

A Miracle Healing at Medjugorje

Thirteen-year-old Nicola Pacini, who lives with his family near Florence, Italy, had been confined to a wheelchair for five years when his parents decided to take him to visit the Virgin Mary shrine in Medjugorje.

Nicola did not wish to go, however, and he told his parents that he wished them to save the money that such a trip would cost. It would be useless to go. It would only bring all three of them additional heartache and disappointment.

Nicola argued that he saw himself as but one of millions of cripples in the world—and he would be but one of thousands of pilgrims who would be crowding around the statue of Mother Mary praying for a healing. Why would they think that the Queen of Heaven would choose him before all the others?

But in December 1991, Nicola agreed to accompany his parents to the holy place where Mother Mary had appeared wearing a crown of twelve stars.

The bus trip was exhausting, but when the Pacini family arrived at the shrine on December 8, Nicola's mother wasted no time in pushing his wheelchair directly in front of Mary's life-size statue.

Perhaps more to please his parents than to get a miracle, Nicola began to pray.

Then, to his astonishment and his parents' great joy, he felt his paralyzed right hand slowly open.

Encouraged by such a marvelous sign of divine energy, Nicola eagerly returned to the shrine the next morning. In his prayers, however, he asked that his healing not be done for his sake alone, but also for that of his parents'.

That being said, Nicola stated that he simply felt like getting up and walking—for the first time in five years.

It was the strangest feeling, Nicola would say later. It was as if something was moving inside him, and he had an overwhelming urge to get up and walk.

And then an "irresistible force" was pushing him to get up from the wheelchair in which he had spent the last five years.

Although he thought that it was impossible, he found himself standing upright—and walking!

After he had taken the first few steps, he called out to his mother and heard her cry of joy that a miracle had occurred.

Mrs. Pacini instinctively rushed to her son's side to help him, but Nicola asked her to leave him alone. He knew that he would walk on his own.

The Pacini family will always remember how the hundreds of pilgrims around the shrine burst into applause when Nicola kept walking.

The boy's mind was filled with the wonder of it all. Mother Mary had heard his prayers and those of his parents.

When the Pacinis returned to Florence, Dr. Rosella Mengonzi, Nicola's physician, was shocked when she saw him standing and walking before her. Although a compassionate individual, Dr. Mengonzi was certain that Nicola would be forced to spend his life in a wheelchair.

After a thorough examination Dr. Mengonzi told journalist Silvio Piersanti, "Nicola Pacini has completely recovered from an incurable disease [muscular dystrophy], and I cannot explain it medically."

Nicola's parents said that their son seemed to be making up for lost time after they had returned from Medjugorje. "He is always romping with his friends. He won't keep still for a minute."

The Pacinis' parish priest, Father Angelo Meliani, informed the press that the Vatican was investigating Nicola's cure before declaring it an official miracle.

Father Angelo said that he personally had no doubts that the healing of young Nicola Pacini was a miracle of Mother Mary's healing love.

He Had to Find Time for Mother Mary's Healing Love after Being Suddenly Struck Blind

Truck driver Ray De La Cruz of Arizona told us that he had experienced his own miracle of healing from the love of Mother Mary, and he had no need to prove it to either medical or church officials.

In November 1990, he was sitting in his rig at an intersection in Mesa, Arizona, just coming back from a long run to Portland, Oregon. He was eager to get home after a hard five days on the road, and he idly raced the engine of his truck as he waited for the red light to change.

As a line of pedestrians crossed the intersection in front of him, Ray De La Cruz glanced at his wristwatch, once again admiring the turquoise band that his wife, Renee, had given him for his fiftieth birthday in July.

"All of a sudden my eyes started to cloud with a gray mist," Ray said. "I didn't know what was happening to me. My surroundings began to dim, and I prayed for the light to change fast so that I could pull my rig over to the side of the road.

"Pretty soon I couldn't even see the traffic lights, and only the horns honking behind me told me that I could drive across the intersection. Somehow I managed to pull my truck and trailer off the street—just as I went totally blind!"

Ray admitted that he was frightened. "I really felt panic. I didn't know what had happened to me."

Sadly enough, neither did the doctors at the clinic. "Renee accompanied me when I went for a battery of tests, because I wanted her there to hear everything and try to understand anything that I might miss," Ray said.

The examining doctors dismissed Ray's fear of a brain tumor or any number of dire physical conditions, but they remained puzzled as to the cause of his sudden blindness.

"Renee told them that I never even complained of headaches. How could this happen just all of a sudden?

"And I had no headache or any pain when the doctors were examining me. I just couldn't see!"

Finally one doctor said in frustration, "Mr. De La Cruz, probably the only thing that can restore your eyesight is a miracle. We cannot find anything medically wrong with your eyes or anything that could have caused your sudden onset of blindness."

Ray endured his sightlessness for nearly six months before Renee said that was enough.

"She began to pray to Mother Mary to lift the shutters from my eyes. And I began to pray also. We asked our daughters, Michele and Teresa, to pray with us. For one entire night, from eight o'clock in the evening to eight o'clock the next morning, we prayed and said the rosary."

Then, about eight o'clock the following evening, Ray came down with a fever.

"I felt like I was burning up. And then it seemed as though there was a bright fire all around me. I mean, I could see red, as if flames were dancing around me. I got hotter and hotter, and I felt like I was in Hell. I started screaming to Mother Mary for help. I shouted for her to come save me from the fires of Hell."

Ray lay back on the bed while Renee placed a cool cloth on his forehead.

"And then I saw Mother Mary somehow, I guess, in my inner eye. She wore a blue gown, a white veil, and she held a rose in her right hand. She smiled at me—and then she disappeared."

When Ray told Renee that he had seen the Holy Mother, she became very excited and asked one of the girls what time it was. "I want to write down a record of this," she said.

In spite of his blindness, Ray had continued to wear his wristwatch due to habit.

"And when Renee asked Michele what time it was, I looked at my wristwatch. And my eyes suddenly started to focus on my watch. Within a few moments I could see clearly the numerals on the watch dial and the pattern of the turquoise watchband that Renee had given me. I could see!"

Overwhelmed with joy, Ray leaped from his bed and kissed and embraced his wife and daughters. "I can see! I can see! Mother Mary has restored my sight!"

Later that night, Ray and his wife sat down on the sofa to think about what had just occurred. "I know there is a lesson and a teaching in this," Renee said.

Ray agreed. "We thought for a long time, and then I said, 'Wait! Think of this: My sight left me when I looked at my watch at the intersection—and it returned when we wanted to see what time it was that I had the vision of Mother Mary.' It has something to do with time, I know it."

The two of them thought and prayed about the mystery through most of another night—and by morning they felt they had the answer.

When Ray got out of the service, he didn't have "time" to go back to school.

He could never find the "time" to get married until he was in his late thirties.

Although Renee was ten years younger than he, they had put off having children, because Ray kept insisting that "it was not yet the right time." Now Ray was fifty, Renee was nearly forty, and their daughters were only nine and seven. Michele and Teresa needed a father who would spend "time" with them.

Ray always complained that he didn't have "time" to help in the house, to maintain the yard, to play with the girls, to go to church, to visit his parents, because he had to keep long hours behind the wheel of his truck. And yet he was the one who kept volunteering for the long hauls.

"To get more money to pay the bills!" he said in his defense.

"But we could get by on less money, if we had more of Papa," Renee countered.

Ray felt pressured. "I have to make money now. I'm fifty. I don't know how much more time I have left behind the wheel."

Time.

"And how much time do you have left with the girls before they are grown and married and off on their own?" Renee challenged him. "How much time do you have left before we are too old to enjoy each other? How much time do we have left before Mother Mary calls you—or me—home? And how much time are we really wasting by watching television or playing cards with our friends when we could be having more quality time together or working more for spiritual goals?"

Ray had no argument against such charges. "You are right, dear one. Mother Mary has given me another chance to have more time with my family and the things that really matter in life. She had to take away my sight so that I might truly see!"

Ray De La Cruz has enjoyed full vision ever since. He quit his job driving the big rigs across country and went to work as a dispatcher for a taxi service. He is home every evening for dinner, and he spends time in constructive activities with his family. He has found time to attend church services regularly and to volunteer in charitable activities. He truly enjoys complete vision.

An interesting footnote: Before he mysteriously lost his sight, he required bifocal lenses in his glasses. Since the visitation of Mother Mary, he has not needed eyeglasses at all.

She Delivered a Healing Message for Mother Mary

In a previous chapter, Clarisa Bernhardt told the story of her first encounter with Mother Mary. Her second meeting with the Holy Mother occurred twenty years later, when "in the middle of a very busy morning with lots of telephone calls," she had a sudden thought of Stevie, the sister of her close friend, Toni.

"Actually, I had only met Stevie on one occasion, about fourteen years before, although we had spoken a few times on the phone," Clarisa explained. "But when I get a strong feeling or an intuitive message, I don't question it. I just try to follow through."

Toni, who had learned to be respectful of her friend's psychic sensitivity, immediately gave Clarisa her sister's telephone number.

The phone rang numerous times. Clarisa was about to replace the receiver when Stevie answered, explaining that she had just walked through the door.

"Are you all right?" Clarisa asked. "I just had the strongest feeling that I must call you."

Very quietly Stevie said that she had just returned from her doctor, who had diagnosed her as having cancer.

"Stevie attempted to laugh, saying she shouldn't be surprised that I would pick up on her bad news," Clarisa said. "I offered her encouragement, and I assured her that I would remember her in my meditations and prayers. Under the circumstances, we had a pleasant phone visit, and I promised her that I would stay in touch."

In spite of a hectic schedule, Clarisa remembered to call Stevie over the next several weeks, "but I always missed her. And she never returned my calls."

The weeks became months. Toni said that her family hoped for the best for Stevie, but they were most concerned about her children.

A day or so later, as Clarisa stepped into the empty elevator at her high-rise apartment building, she was thinking of Stevie. "I sent her a thought of light and love, but then sought to clear my mind of all thoughts, as I had a very busy day ahead of me."

As the elevator began to descend, Clarisa began to notice with her peripheral vision that she was not alone in the elevator.

"A being was standing to my left. It was the beautiful lady that I had seen in the theatre that November day in Los Gatos, California. I recognized her at once. She once again wore a white robe with the cowl covering her hair.

"Suddenly there was a light that became more and more brilliant—until it was as if I were surrounded by this magnificent glow. And then the light seemed to permeate my entire being. I knew without a doubt that it was Mary, the Holy Mother.

"As the light became more and more brilliant, I knew that I was being spoken to . . . that I heard with all my being . . . with all my mind and my heart, the following words: *'Tell Stevie that because of the concern for her children, I will try to intervene and see if I can help with her healing condition.'*"

And then, Clarisa told us, the light was gone. Mary was no longer visible. The elevator reached the main floor, and the door opened to the lobby.

Clarisa knew what she must do. She got back into the elevator to return to her apartment and telephone Stevie with the good news that the Holy Mother wished to help an earthly mother.

Stevie was actually in the midst of a treatment when Clarisa managed to track her down at a hospital in Los Angeles.

"It was no surprise to me to learn later that Stevie's cancer had entered remission," Clarisa said. "She said that after I had relayed Mary's message, she felt uplifted during her entire treatment. She seemed to start feeling good at once. She just seemed to 'float off somewhere' where she had no further pain."

Clarisa rejoiced in her friend's healing and the fact that Mother Mary had helped Stevie in order to bless her children.

A year later, she was once again directed to call Stevie, and she was saddened to learn that the cancer had returned in another area of her body.

"I reminded her about the original message from

Mother Mary," Clarisa said, "and I received intuitively that some good things would be happening for her children."

Since that time, Clarisa was happy to add, both of Stevie's sons had received opportunities to continue in sports on the professional level.

Stevie herself has been able to have the metal "iron cradle" removed that her doctors had implanted to hold her neck straight. She is also once again able to drive, and she has begun to gain weight.

"It does indeed appear to me that Mary the Holy Mother was able to intervene in Stevie's behalf," Clarisa concluded. "And there has been some degree of a miracle made manifest. As for my part in this—well, we certainly can't be all things to all people, but sometimes we can help to deliver a message!"

Mary Heals with a Scent of Roses

Our astrologer friend Barbara May of Tucson, Arizona, shared a beautiful story of the healing of her infant daughter's viral pneumonia through the grace of Mother Mary.

"It was in January 1960 that my four-month-old daughter, Laura, was admitted to the City of Hope Hospital in Duarte, California," Barbara said. "At that time it seemed as though most admissions were done with the understanding that there was little hope of the patient recovering. Laura was admitted with viral pneumonia in both lungs, and we were given little promise that she could be saved."

The infant was placed on the critical list for six days with private nurses in attendance around the clock.

On the afternoon of the sixth day, Barbara felt that she needed a break from the stress of being at her daughter's bedside and went to see the woman who is now her ex-mother-in-law.

"She suggested that we walk to her local parish church in Sierra Madre to pray," Barbara recalled. "She remained at the back in one of the pews, and I went up to the front, to the Our Lady side of the church. I lit a candle and began to pray."

Laura is Barbara's second daughter, and she could not bear to accept the reality of her dying.

"I was asking for grace and understanding," she said. "I remember looking up at the statue of Our Lady and thinking that it must be because of my lack of sleep that the statue appeared to be expanding and glowing."

At the same time, Barbara remembered, "the church was suddenly filled with an almost overwhelming scent of roses that became so powerful that it was nearly sickening.

"I thought at first that only I noticed the scent, but as I walked toward the back of the church, my mother-in-law asked me where the roses were, and she began looking around to see where they might be."

Barbara told us that she can still recall the hush of the church, the afternoon light falling right where they stood, and the strong, enveloping scent of roses.

"My mother-in-law told me that St. Teresa of Liseux had the identical experience with the scent of roses when she prayed to the Virgin Mary," Barbara said.

"I did not see the Virgin, but the smell of roses stayed with me until the next morning, when the hospital called and told me that a miracle had occurred: Laura's fever had broken, and she no longer had any trace of a virus or any pneumonia."

When Barbara returned to the hospital that she had left only ten hours before, she found a rosy-cheeked, healthy baby "whose light brown baby fuzz had turned completely white during the night."

Barbara was so excited that Laura was going to live that it was some time before her mother-in-law reminded her of what had happened that day in church.

"It gave me goose bumps then, and it still does, because I believe that the Virgin Mary answered my prayers that day. I know what I experienced, and I had a witness in my ex-mother-in-law. Most of all, in Laura's miraculous recovery I have a result that is undeniable and documented."

Barbara provided us with an interesting footnote to the above experience vis-à-vis the scent of roses.

"In July 1989 here in Tucson, I was clinically dead for three minutes and forty-three seconds following bowel surgery. This occurred in post-op, and when I 'came back,' a surgical nurse noted that I had talked about a strong scent of roses and that I had asked her if she had smelled it, too. She had—and she said nothing like that had ever happened to her before. As you know, post-op rooms in all hospitals are sterile—and there surely aren't any roses in there."

But it would seem that the Blessed Mother had chosen once again to intercede on Barbara May's behalf and grant her another miracle.

CHAPTER 13

Our Lady Visits
Knock, Ireland

In the late 1880s, the village of Knock in County Mayo, Ireland, was in the midst of a terrible famine. Fifteen devout villagers gathered in the little Catholic church in the village to ask for deliverance from the unrelenting pangs of hunger that had weakened them all.

Then, at one end of the small church, they were amazed to see a glowing light beginning to form.

As the astonished villagers gazed spellbound at the brilliant light, they were able to distinguish the figures of Mother Mary, St. Joseph, and St. John. In the vision the villagers beheld, the holy figures stood at an altar and looked upward at a lamb surrounded by golden stars.

A short time after the villagers had reported their vision, many ill, diseased, or crippled people who visited the church began to claim miraculous cures as they knelt at the statue of the Virgin Mary.

Ecclesiastical authorities from the Roman Catholic Church were sent to investigate the alleged vision and the cures ascribed to the holy visitation. After they had spent several days interrogating the villagers of Knock, the clerics' official conclusion stated that they were convinced that an authentic manifestation of the Blessed Mother had occurred.

Since that time the small village of Knock has come to be called the "Irish Lourdes," and medical authorities continue to be astounded by the number of healings that have taken place at the little church's shrine.

In the 1960s, Nicholas Doyle of Bray County was stricken with rheumatic fever when he was just a boy of ten. Doctors said that the boy's heart had been so severely affected that, in addition to being forbidden to participate in even the mildest forms of exercise, Nicholas had to be confined to his bed. He was denied even the almost negligible exertion of knitting as a means to pass the time.

Just a few days after he had been blessed before the statue of the Blessed Mother in the tiny village church in Knock, Nicholas was riding his bicycle. The Doyles' family doctor found himself completely at a loss to explain the miraculous cure.

Bridie Hopkins, a Leeds teenager who suffered from a diseased leg bone, was another example of a miracle healing. She testified that after she had received the blessing at the shrine in Knock, the numbness in her leg disappeared and there came a strange kind of prickling sensation.

Four months later, doctors pronounced Bridie's leg completely healed.

In the autumn of 1994, Dr. Patrick O'Mara stated that the miraculous recovery of Marion Carroll from multiple sclerosis defied "the laws of science and medicine."

Although Mrs. Carroll, a resident of Athlone, Ireland, began having symptoms of M.S. in 1972, the disease wasn't diagnosed in the young mother until 1978. By then she had lost the use of both of her legs.

Her husband, Jimmy, got her an electric wheelchair, but her hands soon became too weak to work the control button.

Then the muscles in her throat were stricken, and she couldn't speak or swallow properly. She had to drink with a straw, and she was unable to hold her head up without a neck brace.

When it seemed that things could not be worse, Marion developed epilepsy and kidney infections.

Her husband and her two children took turns washing, changing, and feeding her.

Then, on September 3, 1989, forty-one-year-old Marion agreed to allow some friends to take her by ambulance to the statue of the Virgin Mary at Knock. After all, she reasoned, what did she have to lose? She had heard the priest say that he was already planning what kind words he would say at her funeral.

Marion Carroll was carried into the church on a stretcher and placed under the statue.

"I didn't have the heart to pray," she told journalist Fleur Brennan. "I just said to Mary, 'You're a mother, too. You know how I feel about leaving my husband and children.' "

A few minutes later, during a religious service in the village church, Marion felt a strange sensation moving over her. She knew that some unseen force was urging her to walk.

She didn't want to make a spectacle of herself before the statue of the Blessed Mother, so she waited until she had been carried out of the church before she convinced her nurse to undo the straps on her stretcher.

Immediately Marion was propelled to her feet by that same unseen force.

"I was filled with love," she said. "As I stood, I started crying tears of joy."

When Marion Carroll returned home and showed her husband and children that she could walk, there were many more tears of joy and thanksgiving. Jimmy told her that he had been earnestly praying that she would receive a cure.

Dr. Patrick O'Mara, the Carrolls' regular physician, together with a physical therapist, conducted a thorough examination of Marion and declared that the muscles which had been shriveled for eleven years were now totally normal. In addition, the epilepsy and kidney problems that had so afflicted her had also disappeared.

Although patients suffering from multiple sclerosis do have remissions, they generally take place over a period of time, Dr. O'Mara told Fleur Brennan in November 1994. "This was different, because Marion Carroll regained her full health instantly, and she has now been perfectly healthy for five years. I cannot explain what happened."

Dr. O'Mara reinforced his earlier diagnosis and treatment and stated that Marion Carroll's multiple sclerosis was as bad as any that he had ever seen—and she did not have long to live. "But now she is healthy, strong, and energetic."

Our Lady of Knock had worked another miracle.

Steps Taken to Authenticate a Miracle

The Roman Catholic Church is well aware that most miracles are born in the hearts of believers and require no blessing or approval from an ecclesiastical hierarchy to continue to grow in their individual meaning to other pilgrims.

Fr. Frederick Jelly, professor of systematic theology at Mount Saint Mary's Seminary in Emmitsburg, Maryland, has served on miracles committees and has listed the questions asked to authenticate a miracle as the following:

- What is the psychological state of the person claiming the miracle?
- Is there a profit motive behind the miracle claim?
- What is the character of the person who is claiming the miracle?
- Does the miracle contain any elements contrary to scripture or faith?
- What are the spiritual fruits of the miracle—does it attract people to prayer or to acts of greater charity?

Once these questions have been determined and reviewed, the committee makes its decision as to whether or not the event was heavenly inspired. If the committee decides the event is miraculous and its implications have national or international effect, the case may be referred to the Vatican's Sacred Congregation for the Doctrine of the Faith in Rome. The Sacred Congregation has the authority to institute a new investigation and make its own ruling and recommendation to the pope, who is the final arbiter of miracles.

CHAPTER 14

Italy's Weeping
Madonna

She was a flimsy, foot-high madonna cast in hollow plaster
and painted with bright blotches of cheap paint. Her face
was an expressionless glob of vivid pinkness. In her crudely
shaped, pudgy fingers, the little statue tenderly held a
bleeding heart painted in red and gold.

She was like thousands of other plaster madonnas
manufactured at a plant in Sicily and sold throughout the
country for a few lira.

And like so many of the other statues, this particular
madonna was sold as a wedding present when an earnest
friend decided that such a holy statue would be an apt gift
for Antionetta and Angelo Iannuso, who were married in
Syracuse, Sicily, in the spring of 1953.

Dark-haired and attractive, twenty-year-old Antionetta
was a very religious girl who carefully followed the instructions of her church. On the other hand, Angelo, her husband, was a farm laborer who was an admitted communist
sympathizer who had nothing to do with the teachings of
the Roman Catholic Church.

A few months after receiving the statue of the madonna
as a gift, the commotion began in the Iannuso household.

Antionetta became pregnant, and her body was wracked
with agonizing pain. Her vision dimmed, and she suddenly

found it difficult to perform even the easiest of household tasks. Antionetta prayed devoutly to the Blessed Mother to grant her salvation from the torment.

On the morning of August 29, 1953, Antionetta was afflicted with a painful seizure. Her abdomen twisted agonizingly, and her eyes clouded.

It was then that she glanced up at the madonna and saw tears streaming down her cheeks.

"I suddenly thought that I had lost my mind," she said. "But I could see that the statue was weeping like a child."

Forgetting her pain, Antionetta dashed from the bedroom, shouting, "The little madonna is weeping!"

Her mother and sister-in-law were skeptical. One whispered to the other that the pregnant Antionetta was hysterical. They tried to calm the young mother-to-be, and finally, yielding to her insistent demands, examined the little madonna.

Later, both women were to testify that "the tears were so plentiful that they flowed down the face and over into the hand holding the heart. It was the most astonishing thing we have ever seen."

Aloof from religious hysteria and materialistically secure in his atheistic philosophy, Angelo laughed at the story of the plaster madonna weeping tears until he witnessed the phenomenon for himself—a virtual torrent of tears. (Angelo became so moved by the supernatural experience that a few months later he would forsake communism altogether and devoutly assist the local priest as he said mass over the weeping madonna.)

A doubting neighbor removed the madonna from the wall in an effort to discover some "rational, scientific" explanation for the seemingly miraculous occurrence.

"I found absolutely no moisture on the wall," he later reported to journalists. "Later I unscrewed the statue from its base. It was thoroughly dry on the inside. I wiped the madonna dry and I dried the whole figure thoroughly. Within a few seconds, two pearl-like drops glistened in the madonna's eyes."

When the news of the miracle madonna spread throughout Italy, thousands of people hurried to see the weeping statue. Although Syracuse is a bustling Ionian seaport with a population of sixty thousand, the southeastern Sicilian community's hotels were quickly swamped with requests for accommodations.

Further credence was given to the statue when the Syracuse Police Department removed the little madonna to their headquarters for safekeeping. As the squad car moved through the streets, a patrolman carefully held the statue on his lap. Soon his jacket was drenched with tears.

A skeptical detective caught several tears in a chemist's vial and, without identifying the liquid, sent the specimen to a police laboratory for analysis.

The next morning, an irritated lab director confronted the detective. "Why did you send the last specimen over? It's nothing more than human tears. Was that your idea of a joke? I am much too busy to waste my time analyzing such substances."

The unusual healing power of the weeping madonna quickly manifested itself. From the moment that Antionetta had first glimpsed the tears, her painful seizures had disappeared. Her vision had cleared and her thudding headaches became a thing of the past.

Other cures soon followed. The crippled, the lame, and the ill from all of Italy soon gathered before the weeping madonna. The tears were caught on a cloth and wiped on the bodies of the afflicted.

A middle-aged man recovered the use of a crippled arm that he had not been able to use for years.

A three-year-old girl was brought to Syracuse by her hopeful parents. Stricken by polio, the golden-haired child's arm was encased in an array of stainless steel braces.

As the mother and father fervently prayed for a miracle, the child's face and arm were brushed with the madonna's tear-stained cloth.

"See, Mommy, I can move my arm!" the child shouted.

The parents of an eighteen-year-old country girl

brought their speechless daughter to Syracuse to visit the weeping madonna.

"She was struck dumb eleven years ago and has not uttered a word since then," the father told reporters gathered around the madonna's makeshift shrine. "Medical doctors have been unable to cure her."

The mute girl's lips were brushed lightly with the cloth wet with the madonna's tears—and the teenager immediately brightened and began to speak.

The madonna's tears ended on the fourth day.

Exactly one month after the little statue had begun weeping for Antionetta, the madonna was carried through the streets of Syracuse at the head of a procession of thirty thousand people. She was devoutly moved to a railroad shed, encased in a glass case, and capped with a bronze cross.

Since that day thousands of pilgrims have flocked to the shrine of the little madonna, including more than a hundred bishops and archbishops and several cardinals. The glass-walled case is surrounded by dozens of crutches and braces that have been left there as silent testimony of hundreds of miracle healings.

Masses are said throughout the day by a local priest. Hopeful that their community would continue to be known as the "Italian Lourdes," the citizens of Syracuse purchased a twelve-acre site and constructed a lattice-type pagoda shrine for the madonna. Large ramps lead up to the entrance, and there is room for twenty thousand pilgrims within the four hundred-foot-high walls. Thirty-six small chapels surround the shrine and await the devout pilgrim.

Thousands travel each year to Syracuse to pray for a healing miracle—and hundreds have been cured.

In a message to the Sicilians in 1958, Pope Pius XII said:

"So ardent are the people of Sicily in their devotion to Mary that who would marvel if she had chosen the illustrious city of Syracuse to give a sign of her grace?"

CHAPTER 15

Archangel Michael Joins Mary at Garabandal, Spain

On June 18, 1961, four young girls were playing on the outskirts of the small village of San Sebastian de Garabandal, Spain, when they heard what they believed to be a loud clap of thunder.

When the startled children looked around for the source of such a strange sound on a cloudless day, they were frightened to see a bright figure that they knew at once must be an angel.

"I am Archangel Michael," the magnificent being declared, thus confirming their first impression.

The girls were awestruck. Later they couldn't even remember if they had crossed themselves.

After all, encountering angels was a bit out of their area of expertise. Conchita Gonzalez, Maria Dolores Mazon, Jacinta Gonzalez, and Maria Cruz Gonzalez had come to the area to play, not to have a mystical experience. Maria Cruz was only eleven; the other three girls were twelve. They were all from very poor families, and in spite of the common factor of the Gonzalez surname, none of the girls were related.

So Conchita, Maria Dolores, Jacinta, and Maria Cruz did nothing but stand and stare at the heavenly figure until Archangel Michael faded from view.

That remarkable experience would probably have lasted the village girls for life, but Michael appeared to them many times throughout the month of June. Finally he promised them that on July 2 they would be able to meet the Blessed Mother herself.

Located in the northern part of Spain in a rugged area of the Picos de Europa Mountains, the population of Garabandal at that time was only about three hundred souls. There was no doctor in the village, nor was there a resident priest. But there were dozens of the devout and the curious who vowed that they would accompany the four girls to the spot where Archangel Michael had predicted Mother Mary would appear.

At six in the evening, the girls walked to the area to keep their important appointment. In a short time, according to the young revelators, the Holy Mother appeared in the company of two angels, one of whom was Archangel Michael.

The girls went into ecstatic states, and witnesses declared that their little faces reflected the light that they claimed to behold around the Blessed Mother.

They described Mother Mary as dressed in a white robe with a blue mantle and a crown of golden stars. They said that her hands were slender. Her hair, deep nut brown, was parted in the middle. Her mouth was very pretty, and she had a fine nose.

To their eyes, she appeared to be a young woman of about eighteen, rather tall. And the girls excitedly agreed that there was no voice in the world like hers.

And, of course, that was true, for there was no woman in the world like the Blessed Mother, either in the voice, the face, or anything else. Mother Mary had manifested herself, the girls said, as Our Lady of Carmel.

During 1961 and 1962, Mother Mary appeared to the girls a number of times every week. Conchita, Maria Dolores, Jacinta, and Maria Cruz were not always at the apparition site as a quartet. On many occasions only one of the girls would be present to welcome the Blessed Mother.

The schedule of manifestations had also become irregular, ranging from mornings to afternoons to later in the evening.

But whenever the visitations occurred, villagers and pilgrims alike could clearly see the girls entering into ecstatic, or deep trance, states that could last from a few minutes to many hours.

Numerous eyewitnesses said that the faces of the little visionaries revealed an extraordinary sweetness when they were enraptured by the Blessed Mother. It was as if they were transformed by an inner light and their beautiful faces were reflecting a holy glow from a divine spark within.

It was observed by many that the girls seemed transported to a dimension of reality where time did not matter. They never gave the slightest sign of fatigue or discomfort, in spite of the fact that they might be kneeling on rocks with their heads violently thrown backward. On cold days the children came barefoot in the snow to listen for hours to the messages of Mother Mary.

At first there were thoughtless, insensitive skeptics who, during the children's period of ecstasy, would hit them, burn them with matches, or stick them with needles. None of these cruel stimuli elicited the slightest physical response from any of the four girls.

On one occasion an inconsiderate photographer flashed powerful beams of light in the revelators' eyes that under normal circumstances would have burned their retinas and perhaps even caused blindness. Their eyes remained wide open and joyful, and none of the girls even blinked.

In an area above the village called the "Pines," the four diminutive mystics beheld an angel who appeared with a golden chalice and asked them to recite the Confiteor, the prayer of general confession. The girls did as they were instructed, and the angel gave them Holy Communion.

On May 2, 1962, the angel told Conchita that God would perform a miracle and allow the Sacred Host to be seen on her tongue as she received the wafer during the angelic communion service. The date for this miracle, the heavenly being said, would be July 18.

Thousands arrived to witness the holy miracle. Conchita remained isolated in her home until midnight. She was already in a state of ecstasy when she left her home to walk to the Pines. The crowd parted for her, then filed behind in the little girl's footsteps.

At the appointed place and the designated moment, Conchita dropped to her knees, opened her mouth, and put out her tongue to receive the Sacred Host.

As excited pilgrims drew near with lanterns and flashlights, photographer Don Alejandro Daminas, who was standing only three feet from Conchita, was able to get clear pictures of the wafer materializing on the twelve-year-old revelator's tongue.

Those who witnessed the miracle stressed the point that Conchita's arms were at her side the entire time. Never did she raise her hands to her mouth to "palm" a communion wafer on her tongue.

Journalist Benjamin Gomez commented that Conchita's face at that moment of the angelic distribution of the host was "beautifully transformed into heavenly ecstasy." Gomez said that he could certify that the girl was in a motionless state when she received the Sacred Host. "There were many of us who saw this miracle, and we had enough time to contemplate this marvelous phenomenon."

On June 18, 1965, Conchita received a communication from Archangel Michael on behalf of Mother Mary. The Holy Mother had felt so distressed by the content of the message that she could not deliver it herself.

According to Conchita, Michael said many priests were on the road to perdition, and with them they were bringing many souls.

"The Holy Eucharist is being given less importance

and honor in the churches," the Archangel continued. "We must avoid God's anger with us by our efforts at amendment. If we beg pardon with sincerity of soul, He will forgive us.

"I, your Mother, through the intercession of St. Michael the Archangel, want to tell you to amend your lives. You are already receiving one of the last warnings. I love you very much, and I do not want your condemnation.

"Ask us sincerely, and we will give to you. You should make more sacrifices. Think of the Passion of Jesus."

Over a period of nineteen months, the Blessed Mother and Archangel Michael appeared to Conchita or to one or more of the other three girls some two thousand times. Witnesses observed the girls being levitated in their ecstasy, rising as if to kiss or embrace the holy figures. Sometimes they were seen to be lowered slowly backward to the ground, their backs ramrod stiff and straight. Once a large crowd even saw them walking in the air.

A Young Priest Is Granted the Ability to See as the Girls See

One of the strangest of the phenomena associated with the manifestations at Garabandal occurred when a young Jesuit priest named Luis Andreu begged the girls and the Blessed Mother to be granted the ability to behold the wondrous sights that the blessed little ones were permitted to see. At last Father Andreu's request was acknowledged, and he was given permission to participate in a holy visitation.

Although the thousands who assembled that day to watch the simple farm girls in their ecstasy, conversing with the unseen holy personages, were able to see no angel or Holy Mother, for reasons unfathomed Father Andreu became the single exception who was permitted to gaze upon the celestial beings as clearly as Conchita and her friends.

The healthy, robust young priest left Garabandal fervently proclaiming his great, ineffable joy.

To a number of his fellow clerics he spoke of his great blessing and assured them that the supernatural life was not to be feared. He urged them to treat the Blessed Mother and the angelic visitors with the same openness as did the children of Garabandal. He declared Conchita and her fellow little visionaries to be examples for them all.

Within thirty-six hours of his remarkable interaction with Mother Mary and Archangel Michael, Fr. Luis Andreu died in the midst of exclaiming to a friend that he had just experienced the happiest day of his life.

Doctors at the clinic who examined the young priest's body stated that they could find no discernable causes for the healthy man's sudden demise.

His fellow priests simply stated that Luis had died of joy.

Conchita Gonzalez received her final visitation from Mother Mary on November 13, 1965, and the Queen of Heaven left her young prophet with a mystery to announce to the world. Conchita said that she had been given the date of a mighty miracle that would be performed on a Thursday at 8:30 P.M.—but she was not permitted to reveal the date until *eight days* before it was to occur.

Conchita said Mother Mary had promised her that before the miracle took place, all humankind would receive a warning from Heaven directly from God. It will be visible to the entire world, and it will be seen and felt by all people, regardless of their religion, believer and unbeliever alike.

If the world did not take heed of Our Lady's warning messages at Garabandal, Conchita went on to state, punishment would be visited upon the entire planet after the miracle has occurred.

Although she said that she could not reveal exactly what kind of punishment would be dealt to the world, it would be "a result of the direct intervention of God."

When Conchita was shown a preview of the awful

chastisement that would be humankind's fate if the warnings of Mary were ignored, she urged everyone to repent quickly. Conchita said that she felt great fear when she saw the terrible chastening, even though the Blessed Mother was at her side.

CHAPTER 16

Mary Is Seen at Zeitoun, Egypt, for Three Years

On April 2, 1968, two mechanics working in a city garage across the street from St. Mary's Church of Zeitoun, Egypt, were startled to see what appeared to be a nun dressed in white standing on top of the large dome at the center of the roof.

"What is the sister doing up so high?" one of the men asked the other in an excited tone. "Something is not right about this."

The other mechanic was in wholehearted agreement. "See how she clings to the stone cross at the top of the dome. She wavers, as if . . ."

His companion grabbed his forearm, cutting off his words and fears. "Dear God," he gasped, voicing his terrible thoughts, "you don't think that she wishes to commit suicide? You don't think she intends to leap to her death?"

The two mechanics decided not to waste another moment with their fearful speculation. One of them ran into the church to get a priest; the other telephoned for a police emergency squad.

When the priest ran from the church to look up at the dome in the center of the roof, he was the first to recognize the remarkable event for what it truly was, a manifestation of Mother Mary.

The now glowing white image of the Blessed Mother remained in full view of the priest, the two mechanics, and a growing crowd of excited witnesses for several minutes, then disappeared.

The news of the Holy Mother's visitation spread rapidly from Zeitoun, a suburb of Cairo, to the greater metropolitan population of over six million. While it is true that the religious makeup of Cairo is largely Muslim, there exists a fairly large Coptic Catholic minority. Thousands began to gather around the majestic church of Zeitoun at Tomanbey Street and Khalil Lane to see for themselves the Queen of Heaven come to Earth.

When Mother Mary came again to rest upon the dome of the church on April 3, a large crowd of men and women were there to greet her with awed shouts of jubilation and whispered prayers of supplication. As if responding to such a devout and enthusiastic reception, she returned to the church on April 9.

Amazingly, the visions of the Holy Mother manifested sporadically atop the dome of St. Mary's Church at Zeitoun for three years. Millions witnessed the visitations, and numerous photographs of the spiritual phenomenon are in existence.

The apparitions were most often heralded by mysterious lights, which were said to flash somewhat in the manner of sheet lightning. These unusual displays of illumination would continue for about fifteen minutes before the Madonna herself would appear in a brilliant burst of light.

According to witnesses, these peculiar lightning-like flashes would manifest sometimes above the church and at other times in the strange clouds that occasionally formed over St. Mary's.

It was frequently reported that these formations of clouds would take shape over the dome from a sky that only a brief time before had been clear and completely free of even a wisp of a cloud.

On one occasion Bishop Gregorius declared that the clouds were formed of incense, admittedly of such a quantity that millions of censers could not produce their equal. The perfumed clouds descended from atop the dome and settled over the multitudes encircling the church, who also bore testimony to the scented blessing.

Another aspect of the phenomenon reported by witnesses was the mysterious appearance of glowing, bird-like creatures, which would often materialize both before and after the apparition of Mother Mary.

According to numerous journalists who traveled from all over the world to record the miraculous series of phenomena in Zeitoun, the entities resembled glowing white doves. Other observers argued that the airborne beings were larger than doves, more the size of pigeons.

Since neither bird is known to fly at night, the devout pilgrims spoke out to settle the debate—the creatures could not be any kind of natural bird. Perhaps they were angels.

They could not be any kind of ordinary bird, stated one account of the mysterious, illuminated birds because, first of all, they flew too rapidly—and without ever moving their wings. They were spotless, emitting white light, and they appeared to glide before, into, and around the image of Mother Mary. They materialized, appeared, and disappeared without any sound at all.

In his book *Our Lady Returns to Egypt*, Rev. J. Palmer documents the various attitudes of the Blessed Mother as she manifested atop St. Mary's dome:

> At first she appeared above the dome in traditional form, wearing the veil and long robes associated with other appearances, such as at Lourdes and Fatima. . . .
>
> Mary does not stand motionless, but is seen bowing and greeting the people in silence. She bends from the waist, moves her arms in . . . blessing and sometimes holds out an olive branch to the people.

Rev. Palmer, an American priest who traveled to Cairo to witness the miracle for himself, stated that Mary was seen to appear:

between the trees in the courtyard in front of the church; she has appeared under each of the four small domes, through the windows of the larger dome, and has often walked on the flat church roof so as to be seen by those standing on all sides of the church.

The visions of the Blessed Mother continued to manifest at the church at Zeitoun from 1968 through 1971. The duration of her visits varied greatly, from a few minutes to several hours. One evening in June 1968, she was viewed from 9:00 P.M. to 4:30 A.M.

Although thousands of people claimed miraculous cures as they looked upward at the glowing figure of the Holy Mother, no one announced any special messages from Mary. There were no warnings of impending Earth changes, no admonitions to repent or to cease sinning. Neither were there any predictions, secret or otherwise.

Strangely enough, Mary chose to remain silent from her majestic and commanding pulpit atop the church in Cairo. It was as if her very presence provided the most powerful proof possible to both believer and unbeliever alike that she does exist in a kingdom beyond our own—yet she is always accessible to those who call upon her name and her love.

CHAPTER 17

The Return of the Great Mother Goddess

In the May 1995 issue of the *Omega New Age Directory*, Rev. John Rodgers hails the Goddess as "the mother of us all, known and worshipped since humanity's earliest days." Yet, he observes, when he began the publication twenty-five years ago, "religious America was so culturally naive and parochial that few souls could imagine goddess worship beyond the context of some ancient civilization or a group of jungle savages."

Rev. Rodgers rightly comments that the worship of the Goddess has never ceased. "Even under the strict control of Christianity and Islam, worship of her continued. Christians worshipped her as Mary and Moslems worshipped her as Fatima. But once we entered the New Age, worship of the Goddess began openly. The Goddess movement has an estimated 100,000 to 500,000 followers in the U.S. alone . . . having its roots in two other movements—the pagan movement and the feminist movement."

Continuing his overview of the contemporary Goddess movement, Rev. Rodgers makes the valid point that there have always been Goddess-worshippers among the non-Christians and secret devotees within the church, paying homage to the Goddess under a number of different names, such as Isis, Astarte, the Lady, the Mother, Diana, and so forth.

There is no question about the power of the Great Mother archetype. In his classic work on the subject, *The Great Mother: An Analysis of the Archtype*, Erich Neumann writes:

> The primordial mysteries of the Feminine are connected more with the proximate realities of everyday life. . . . In accordance with an essential trait of feminine psychology, the earlier mysteries take place on the level of direct but unconscious experience. . . .
>
> In the primordial mysteries, the Feminine . . . assumes a creative role and so becomes the determining factor in early human culture. Whereas the instinctual mysteries revolve around the central elements in the life of a woman—birth, menstruation, conception, pregnancy, sexuality, climateric, and death—the primordial mysteries project a psychic symbolism upon the real world and so transform it.
>
> The mysteries of the Feminine may be divided into mysteries of preservation, formation, nourishment, and transformation.

Undeniably, in the past thirty years we have been witnessing an increasing number of reports concerning the appearance of the Great Mother image, which, depending upon the witnesses, have been interpreted as the Blessed Mother, Pallas Athena, Isis, or Diana. As report after report crosses our desks, we find ourselves continually asking: Just what can it all mean?

Dr. W. G. Roll, one of the mainstays of the Psychical Research Foundation, Duke Station, Durham, North Carolina, once suggested to us that apparitions of the Blessed Mother and other heavenly beings could also be expressions of what is going on within the self.

"Self, in the proper context, encompasses the world," Dr. Roll explained. "Parapsychology suggests that there is no real distinction between certain levels of experience. There is no distinction between persons and between a person and his physical environment. These things are part of a sort of continuum, the sort of thing that physicists talk about, the space-time continuum.

"But the space-time continuum is not very interesting unless it can be made the object of experience—and this again can happen as the result of any number of procedures, of which the ordinary ones would be meditation, prayer, and other attempts to reach beyond this more narrow ego, or self, that we live with almost every day of our lives."

Dr. Roll reminded us that Carl Jung postulated that in every man's unconscious there exists an anima, a personification of his repressed female attributes. Conversely, every woman possesses an animus, a male principle. In dreams, different aspects of the dreamer's personality are often represented by different people. Therefore, when a man dreams of a female angel, he may simply be perceiving his anima in disguise. In like manner, when a woman dreams of a female angelic entity, her unconscious may be depicting her ideal self.

Are we witnessing the activation of a long-slumbering goddess, the renewed manifestation of a universal archetype, or a kind of externalized anima of the collective unconscious?

The Goddess Has Always Helped Those Who Pay Her Homage

"Diana has always been the benefactress of the outcast, the lonely, the people of the night," Dr. Leo Louis Martello, an *Imago* [male Witch], once told us. "The Goddess has never cared what, or who, you are. Her standards have never been those of any given society. She has always helped those who pay her homage.

"To this day," Dr. Martello went on, "there is a vast underground network of *streghe* [Witches] throughout Italy, Sicily, with allies on Malta, including a few Roman Catholic priests, who accept the Blessed Mother Mary because they know that she is just another incarnation of the goddess Diana. One day we will once again have a public temple to the Goddess."

Dr. Martello is among many critics of Christianity who argue that one of its principal failings lies in its lack of the feminine aspect within the godhead. More than a few observers of the mass conversions of the pagan populace of Europe during the Middle Ages commented that the common folk simply went underground with their worship of Diana, or made the motions of giving reverence to Mary while secretly directing their true devotion to the Goddess.

Dr. Martello had something to say about this as well: "While I was living in Tangier, Morocco, in 1964, I took a three-week trip to Sicily, where I visited relatives and local *streghe*. They knew at once that I was an *Imago*. We visited ancient temple sites, and they showed me how Sicilian witchcraft managed to flourish underground for centuries. For example, close inspection of the madonna and child in the cathedral at Monreale will reveal that the child Jesus is *female*!

"Christianization may have forced the old religionists underground in the twelfth century, but the sculptors still paid tribute to their goddesses Demeter and Persephone by creating the madonna and a female Jesus. In ancient times people from all over the world worshipped at the Temple of Demeter in Enna, Sicily, where they celebrated her daughter Persephone's resurrection from the underworld to become goddess of souls and immortality. To this day the Sicilians worship the female deity more than the male, and every city has its sainted patroness."

The Great Mother and the Rise of Feminism

If it is true that the great masses of humankind hunger to give spiritual expression to a mother as well as a father deity, it could be argued that the many reported appearances of the Mother Mary in the past five hundred or so years of Christianity were the result of a kind of psychic compensation for an orthodox, ecclesiastical emphasis on a male chauvinist Trinity.

Visions of the Madonna do seem most often to appear to women. Could it be that in the so-called Christian nations women have subconsciously felt cheated of a more active role in the Church? A member of the Roman Catholic priesthood is addressed as "Father." However, his female counterpart is not called "Mother." She is relegated to "Sister," differentiated from other women because she has surrendered her individuality to become a bride of Christ. Pope John Paul II stands firm in stressing the Vatican's official opinion that Jesus chose only *male* disciples, thus denying the status of priest to women. And it has only been within the past few years that the major Protestant churches have permitted more than a token number of female pastors and ministers.

When John Godwin was researching his book *Occult America*, he noticed striking parallels between the contemporary interest in personal mysticism and the rise of the women's liberation movement, and he felt strongly that this was no coincidence: "These social currents both represent expressions of resurgent femininity, even though they are two entirely different aspects of it. You could compare them to the opposite wings of an advancing army."

An estimated three-quarters of the twenty million Americans interested in astrology are women. At least sixty percent of all the professional psychics, seers, mediums, and laboratory parapsychologists are women. And while there are a number of prominent male gurus, the vast majority of their disciples are female, and their teachings generally emphasize the feminine aspect of the eternal wheel of yin and yang.

It would be both simplistic and unfair to account for such statistics by suggesting that women by nature are more superstitious than men, more susceptible to illogical premises and the mystical interpretation of reality. As some analysts have theorized, women may have a greater affinity for astrology because of their intimate link with the lunar cycle through their menstrual cycle.

Godwin quotes a practicing Witch named Stephanie who told him that witchcraft, the Old Religion, was immensely attractive to many women because of its matriarchal basis. In her opinion, "every one of the established creeds—Christianity, Islam, Hinduism, Judaism, etc.—is patriarchal, authoritarian, and to some degree anti-feminine. Most of them are also anti-sex; you might say anti-life. To them everything connected with the body—especially a woman's body—is somehow unclean, corrupting to the soul. . . . The Old Religion is a fertility faith. . . . Its primary deity is the Great Earth Mother. . . . And don't forget that every coven is headed by a high priestess—or should be, according to tradition."

Drawing Down the Moon

Margot Adler is a brilliant and articulate Witch who has written such books as *The Resurgence of Paganism in America* and the more recent *Drawing Down the Moon*. Brought up to be a rationalist, Margot began a spiritual search for a belief structure that would present an ecological view of the world, a holistic, spiritual view of Earth. In the early 1970s she visited England one summer and discovered the Craft.

"In the ritual known as 'drawing down the moon,' " Margot once explained to us, "the High Priestess invokes the Goddess, draws the Goddess down into herself, and then, in a sense, becomes the Great Mother."

Margot finds no distinction between the feminist and the ecological response: "I think the tie between feminism and ecology and the Craft is that when we speak of the Earth, we speak of that creative, life-giving force. And when I think of the Mother, or the Goddess, she is in some sense inseparable with all those concepts of the Earth, the greening of the Earth, the getting back to nature. . . . I find that there is a real connection between an ancient, holistic, animistic concept of the Earth, and also an ancient concept of what the feminine is."

How would she define "the feminine"?

"It is very difficult to define because all definitions of it come from a society like ours which is in servitude to programming," Margot answered after a moment's consideration. "It's very easy for me to say that the feminine is that which is creative. The feminine is that which is life-giving. It's very easy for me to say a lot of clichés. I have to say, frankly, that I don't think we will ever really know what is female and what is male until we have the kind of society we are hoping will dawn after the Aquarian Age."

In the October–November 1971 issue of *Cosmos*, an editorial writer introduced a profile of a new age minister, Rev. Betsy Chattaway, with the comment that in the Aquarian Age, woman would return to her role of leader in religion, only she will henceforth be called "reverend" rather than "priestess."

The article states that there have been many civilizations in the past where woman guided the community's homage to God: "In Christianity, woman has always been relegated to the backseat. . . . Woman could bring forth the Christ Child and become a saint, but she could not lead or direct. The best she could do was to become a Mother Superior in a convent, but she was subject to a masculine hierarchy."

The article goes on to say that the Aquarian Age will recognize that all people have within them characteristics of both male and female. There will be a new understanding of the active woman and the passive man: "Androgynous humans, so suppressed before, are being allowed to let their creative energies flow. They truly will prove to be humankind's saviors. Mortals will be led by androgynes into a fuller expression of themselves as they are taught to be what they really are—supernatural."

The Feminine Activating Archetype and the Birth of the Cosmic Person

For a number of years now, Jean Houston has been a powerhouse of creative energy, lecturing, publishing, presenting workshops, exploring the parameters of what it is to be human. With her husband, Robert Masters, Jean has established the Foundation for Mind Research in Pomona, New York, and we remember with great affection the conversation that we once had with Ms. Houston concerning, among other fascinating topics, the return of the Great Mother.

"A being that has been worshipped as a goddess has a certain kind of activating energy in itself," Jean observed. "I think there is emerging in our time—perhaps just to restore the balance of nature—the rise of the feminine in the psyche. This energy is manifesting as the traditional goddesses who have contained a great deal of energy with regard to the activating anima such as Isis or Sekhmet or Mary."

Jean theorized that the feminine activating archetype began shortly after the end of World War II: "That was almost the end of the male activating archetype. Hitler, for example, we see as almost a demonic male archetype gone wrong. *Circa* 1950, we begin to perceive, I think, the entry of the female archetype to restore the balance. You need all the female goddesses you can find, so people are going into Babylonia and into ancient Egypt and into the old Witch female cults."

As an instrument of balance, Jean perceived the activating feminine principle as serving as the cosmic midwife that would bring about the *Parousia*, the cosmic person. And, she emphasized, it is cosmic *person*, not cosmic *man*.

"Man and the symbol for man used to mean, in many languages, just humankind. It was not man *qua* man. It only became differentiated very, very late. The ancient

Scandinavian form of the rune for man was the symbol of the female goddess. This symbology was also true in ancient Crete."

Ms. Houston speculated that the planet was approaching a "brief spurt of a female period."

No, she qualified, she was not referring to some kind of matriarchy. "I think there is going to be a period of female music, female psychology, female philosophy, even perhaps a political form. This period may last for fifty to a hundred years. But remember, time is becoming so accelerated that what may normally take two or three thousand years could be over and done with in a few decades.

"And then we are going to move into a new activating archetype, which I think is the cosmic person—humankind in symbiotic relationship to the universe at large. We're going to have a much larger universe."

Mary, the "Chaste Essence" of the Feminine That Balances Human Evolution

In *The Eternal Feminine: A Study on the Text of Teilhard de Chardin*, Fr. Henri de Lubac, a professor of fundamental theology and church history at the Faculty of Catholic Theology, University of Lyons, delineates the great devotion that the brilliant mystical theologian felt toward the ideal of the feminine as epitomized in the Virgin Mary. As did C. G. Jung, de Chardin believed that the feminine element was vital in achieving balance in human evolution.

Teilhard de Chardin saw all the "chaste essence of the Feminine" realized in Mary, and he thereby attributed to her a kind of universality similar to that of Christ.

In consequence, we find in Teilhard, in his piety as in his teaching, a constant parallel between the Son and his Mother. Of both he resolves to "make them more real" in his life. Just as Christ is "Our Lord," so is Mary "Our Lady."

Fr. de Lubac discloses a note written by de Chardin in 1917 in which he establishes a sort of equivalence between "Our Lord, perfect man" and "Our Lady, the ideally pure woman."

> Within the mystical body, he believed, Mary fulfills a "mysterious function which is complementary" to Christ's: for each one of us she serves as the necessary "introducer." Similarly, he establishes a parallel between Our Lord's Ascension and Mary's Assumption. . . . And that is why, like Christ, with whom she is henceforth fully associated, she is "universal": with Christ, "she has filled all things."

Later in his work and writings [*circa* 1940], Teilhard de Chardin saw that devotion to Mary served to satisfy in the Catholic Church the need to correct "a dreadfully masculinized" concept of the Godhead. Although for his own part, de Chardin preferred to think of God and to entrust himself to God "as to a great maternal force," Fr. de Lubac argues that it is unjust to conclude that he wished to make Mary the counterpart of some goddess or to include her in the Divine Trinity. Teilhard de Chardin believed that:

> Like all of us, Mary is a creature; when we consider her in her life on earth, we see her above all as the perfect model of what the creature should be before the face of God. . . . When Teilhard is speaking of the mysteries of the Immaculate Conception and the Annunciation, he urges us to contemplate her in her open, receptive attitude. He also asks us to admire in her the virtues of faith, purity, humility, fidelity, and silence: the "static virtues," which are eminently the Marian virtues.

Sophia, Goddess of Wisdom

In Ecclesiasticus, one of the Deutrocanonical books, Wisdom is identified as feminine, the creative principle that God fashioned first before all things:

> To whom has the instruction of wisdom been revealed and made manifest? And who has understood the multiplicity of her ways? [God] created her in the Holy Spirit, and saw her, numbered her, and measured her. And he poured her out upon all flesh as his gift, and has given her to those who love him. (1:6, 9–10)

Could it be possible that the great Mother archetype that some people have witnessed is, in actuality, an expression of Sophia, Wisdom, herself? Some spiritual scholars believe that may be so.

In the Fall 1989 issue of *Gnosis*, Caitlin Matthews observes that the major mystics of all faiths "have perceived the Lady Wisdom as the bridge between everyday life and the world of the eternal, often entering into deep accord with her purpose."

In her excellent book *Sophia: Goddess of Wisdom*, Ms. Matthews writes, "What with revelatory appearances of the Blessed Virgin all over the firmament and the awkward polemical challenges of amazons and furies upon earth, it is clear even to the most hidebound theologians that something important is going on."

Ms. Matthews wonders about the role of Christian feminists in the Church. Do they remain spiritually in hiding or do they come forth and assume their spiritual ministry openly?

In the spirit of Sophia, she argues, women could assume the roles of prophets, healers, mediators, and counselors. Women could fulfill such spiritual responsibilities with great verve and resource:

if the orthodox barriers could admit the annexing of the ecclesial sanctuary where only men may celebrate the Eucharist. Would new sacraments be devised? Would Woman as Christian priestess administer the rites of healing, reconciliation, death counseling, therapy of the mentally tormented? This would indeed manifest the compassion of Sophia.

Ecclesiasticus 1:15–17 continues to speak of Sophia/ Wisdom as a most high and wonderful blessing of God:

They to whom she reveals herself love her by sight and by the knowledge of her great works. The fear of the Lord is the beginning of wisdom; she is instilled in the faithful in the womb; she walks with chosen women and is known to the just and faithful.

To continue to grow in stature with wisdom is a lifelong process:

My son . . . even to your old age keep finding wisdom. Come to her as one who plows and sows and wait for her harvest. In working for her, you will labor for a little while and will soon eat of her crops. . . . The foolish will not remain with her. She will weigh them down as a heavy testing stone and they will soon abandon her. . . . She is not manifest to many, but with those to whom she is known, she continues faithful. . . .

Listen, son, take my advice. . . . Come to her with all your mind and keep her ways with all your power. Search for her and she will be made known to you; when you have obtained her, do not let her go. In the end, you will find rest in her, and she will be turned into your joy. . . . You will put her on as a robe of glory, and you will set her upon your head as a crown of joy. (Ecclesiasticus 6:18–32)

Our very souls seem to respond to the dualistic dimension of Earth, dividing themselves into the feminine-creative principle and the masculine-guiding principle. It is the feminine aspect that inspires, the masculine aspect that shapes and refines.

And it may be quite possible that from time to time these facets of our souls may assume the archetypal images most suitable and most understandable to the individuals who desire to perceive materially that which they have visualized mentally—and thus a vision of the Great Mother-Sophia-Wisdom may manifest.

The feminine is deeply a part of all of us, and it must be given its proper recognition in our lives. The Holy Spirit is recognized as an expression of the feminine aspect of the Godhead. God the Father is the basic, organizing, and structuring principle in the universe, but God the Mother is the creative energy that inspires all formulations required for the realization of thoughts, words, and deeds.

It should also be noted here that the Greek Muses, those creative entities who manifested to inspire artists, poets, and thinkers, were always depicted as females. And isn't "Necessity" the "mother" of invention?

Elaine Pagels writing in *The Gnostic Gospels* tells of a recently discovered text from Nag Hammadi, *Trimorphic Protennoia* (Triple-formed Primal Thought), that celebrates the feminine principle, the Holy Spirit:

> [I] am ... the Thought that [dwells] in [the light] ... moves in every creature. ... I am the Invisible One within the All. ... I am perception and knowledge, uttering a voice by means of thought. [I] am the real Voice. I cry out in everyone, and they know that a seed dwells within.

In the *Arizona Republic*, priest-author Rev. Andrew Greeley (*The Cardinal Sins*) told religion writer Richard Lessner that the concept of God as a woman had recently seized him and he planned to explore it in a forthcoming novel. Explaining that in Roman Catholic theology Mary reflects the femininity of God, Rev. Greeley said that Catholics needed a more complete awareness of the feminine aspect of God's nature:

> Our research shows that twenty-five percent of those under thirty have thought of God as a woman. This is an idea whose time has come. This will show up in art and literature and will offend some and fascinate others.

CHAPTER 18

The Grandmother Creator Spirit

Volume 1, Issue 2, of *Wolf Lodge Journal* is dedicated to the feminine, the Mother, the Grandmother, the Wisdom Women. When editor Judi Pope asks Brooke Medicine Eagle, author of *Buffalo Woman Comes Singing*, the meaning of "Grandmother and Grandfather," she replies that those terms refer to Mother Earth and Father Spirit. In the same frame of reference, she says, *Great* Grandmother, "like the *Great* Goddess, the *Great Mother* . . . is the Beginning of all things."

After she has added the "next level" down from the Grandmother/Great Mother Spirit, that is, "Grandmothers in the sense of ancestor spirits," Brooke Medicine Eagle speaks of the Grandmothers who are elderly women living today:

> These are the white-haired crone wisdom women who are carrying . . . love and nurturing, and they consciously hold a loving energy in prayer for all of the grandchildren of our relations. They are the women who understand the Grandmother Wisdom Lodge.

A Navajo traditional account of the origin of the totem tells how the Grandmother Creator brought from her home in the West, nine races of original beings—the deer, sand, water, bear, hare, wolf, rattlesnake, tobacco plant, and reed grass—a number of which she eventually transformed into humans.

When the early humans often found it difficult to find enough subsistence in the wild, it was the Grandmother who, seeing her children's need, created domesticated animals for their special use.

Among many of the Eastern tribes, such as those that made up the Iroquois Confederacy, it was the Grandmother of humankind who revealed all the roots and plants of medicine and healing—and it is to the Grandmother that all wise Medicine practitioners make their invocation whenever they take anything from the earth.

As we have said earlier in this book, the Great Mother is a dynamic and powerful figure to whom all peoples, all cultures, all religious expressions—at least on some level of perception and consciousness—feel a strong and emotional obeisance. The Native American spiritual traditions feel an exceptionally intense devotion to the Mother/Grandmother image, and the increasing number of sightings of the Mother throughout the world speak to the individual shaman and practitioner of Medicine as profoundly as the manifestations of Mary touch the heart and soul of the Christian priest and devout parishioner in a manner that circumvents the rational dictates of a scientific age.

In that same excellent issue of *Wolf Lodge Journal*, Marri Parkinson, a psychotherapist and owner of Clarion Gallery on Orcas Island, Washington, states that she is convinced that "there is no hope for this planet unless women . . . claim their power, and from the place of strength learn to balance and harmonize with the males who share this home with us."

In her article, "Hummingbird Speaks," she continues:

> In all due respect to my brothers, the reality is that this is a feminine planet. Mother Earth. Mother

Nature. As women, we are at home here. We are the representation of the planet and ideally serve as a lens for her power and beauty.

In their *Other Council Fires Were Here Before Ours*, Twylah Nitsch and Jamie Sams write:

> In ancient times, the main purpose of nightly Council Fires was to learn how to listen. The truths of how to live in harmony were kept alive by wise Storytellers who would relate tribal wisdom through Medicine Stories to those who would gather to listen around the nightly fires. Tribal tradition, history, acts of courage, and lessons on how to discover the true Self came to life through the events related in the legends of the Ancestors. It was the responsibility of the listeners to relate and apply truths to their personal lives in a manner that would make them grow.

"Come, Listen to the Grandmother Stories"

Lorraine Darr is a well-known and highly respected healer and mystic who now divides her time between Arizona and her native Iowa. On September 15, 1987, she received the first of a series of "Grandmother stories," a kind of transcendent touching of the Great Mother/ Grandmother feminine energy in which she entered an in-between time and an in-between universe and returned with wisdom and truths to share. As a dear friend of many years, Lorraine has agreed to allow us to excerpt a number of these transmissions from the holy circle of Grandmothers.

In correspondence to us, Lorraine explains that the experiences and soul conversations with the Grandmothers were part of her expansion of mind into being:

I was aware of doing these things and watching the doing also. I would image myself standing in front of the Sphinx, humming the tone of B in the scale. Then I would be in the room where the scrolls and discs were on the shelves. There were other rooms with many machines, and I think also some crystals and gemstones.

The band of Light I was given to image for the planet I still use and image. Those discs on the shelves I would pick up, place my fingers alternately on the edge, then with each hand pulling in the opposite direction, the disc became like a Slinky. When my hands stopped, I was holding a scroll to read and feel. To compress it again when finished, I gently pushed the ends together and lay the disc back on the shelf. There were many discs! I did a lot of studying there!

9-15-87: In a Time of Light, we sat in a circle to sound the call of sparkling crystal points. The call went out on waves of vibrant sound to all spaces. Once the waves are sent out, we observe the actions and reactions in our Forms, for in this way we know what the call does to the Light Bodies who receive it. . . .

We know the Earth is prepared well into the Time of No-Time. All souls are in place as the untold streams of sound are connected to these souls for their space of teaching.

Watch closely now as the call touches all things in the Wave of Light movement. Some have remembrances of Light and are aware of Beings of Grace around them. Others are not hearing the Wave or responding. Others are feeling and not knowing. . . .

The Wave has reached its outward space and returns the flow to that which we are. It comes in the silent ONE as we in the circle have become a vibrant scroll of Being. . . .

Soft, supple, and with grace, the scroll opens to reveal the blazing point of light in words of joy and understanding.

My eyes and fingers feel the story, and it swells from my heart.

O soul of Light, come again to the Temple of Joy, for

this is in your true home. Where you are now on Earth is only a place to rest and to see this space of knowing.

Look upon the child with delight, for you have the opportunity to teach the wonders of the universe.

The child has come from the far stars to live and to resonate with the Light. . . .

"Know that you are the child and the story and the light. Speak, child."

Where have I been? Where do I go? What do I know to give, for that is the reason for knowing.

Are you my Mother?

The voices say, "No, child, thy mother is the Earth and the Wind. Thy Father is the Sun and the Suns of Light. We are the Grandmothers who come to the children to teach of the Light and of love. . . .

"By radiating your love, you alter your space upon Earth and become a joyful Space, both inside and out.

"The Grandmothers are connected to you by a golden thread of love for your guidance—if you choose to listen. The Grandmothers know all times and all things under the sun. We have always been the supportive factor of Light for all humans upon Earth.

"Look now upon the pages and chapters in the scroll with a knowing eye, for there you shall hear wave after wave that we have created for humans. . . . There is a common weaving and a song of Light that guides all moments.

"For it is the child who shall bring the man/woman into unity—and thence into being as Lighted Humans. It is the child who leaves the woman to teach all who watch. . . . The child is one with the Grandmothers, and they strengthen the child in every human as it wakes and watches and loves. . . ."

With joy we watch the many lights interact and learn of the joy and laughter and wisdom of the many temples yet to know again fully.

"Be the Children of Light all ways as the Way is shown. . . . So it is, and so it is given from the silken scrolls."

* * *

9-21-87, 12:15 A.M.: I come to sit in the Circle of the Grandmothers as the call came forth to come and to do. . . .

"We begin with a Light to give to the Children of Earth. . . . Listen as the hum surrounds you and fills you and shows you the images of the story. Look upon the screen of mind, children, for now you see a ball with a horizontal circle marked about it. On that circle is placed rows of interlocking double pyramids. In the space where the pyramids meet are rows of points that are coordinated with the core crystal pointed toward the center of Earth. These points are . . . to be put in motion for use in balancing the planet. There is a row, point to point on the Equator or marked circle. Above and below that row are single rows joined to the center row. This creates a band of Light around the planet that acts as a resonating arrangement of points held in complete synchronization with the suns and the solar system patterns. . . .

"Do you remember your chosen path of learning upon the Earth?

"Do you hear the points as they speak to one another?

"Can you see the Lights of both humans and other shapes as they flash and shine?

"As you listen to your heart's voice, you will remember all things and share one with another the universe as you see and hear it. When you see that your heart's voice is the Mother-Father radiant glow, then you will have returned to the circle of the Grandmothers you left long ago.

"We are glad to speak to you and teach you of the life you live when you hear the points of Light. Our blessings and love to you all. . . . We shall sing to you in the wind and smile at you from the flowers. Come again, children. We love you."

Full Moon Night—11-6-87; 12:22 A.M. I see the golden clouds and hear the call of the Grandmothers of the Ancient of Days. I come; I listen; I feel the Circle of Love 'round about me.

"We have come to you, Child of Light, with crystal sound so that you can be a point of Light for our sharing. You read the scrolls clearly, just as you did when they were created."

There is a humming vibration as the scroll opens with care, and I listen to words it speaks:

"See the Crystal Chamber where many gathered to be transformed and transferred to your Earth. Look and fly on the waves of being. . . . First, we have stopped at the Sphinx, and we have joined others in a quiet space for taking on a cloak of sparkling Light.

"From the Sphinx, we go to the Temple of the Sun and collect a headpiece or sphere of sound. Put this on, for it alters the Light to the needed tone and rhythm to pass into the crown space."

We rest in a pulsating shape as the head sphere speaks: "We rejoice, children, in your coming, for there are tales of joy and tales of knowing, as well as stories of transferred understandings to be heard. Watch as the sparkling cloak creates your steps of change and brings the Light to you in many ways.

"Know that the Lighted Grandmothers have taught and formed the knowing space to beings of beings, as well as various waves of humans. For the Earth there was designed a special formation of beings from the stars and spaces to be the preparers and the creators of the now-race of humans. As the Light of humans progressed from cycle to cycle, the complete form was held by us for the full completion of a wave and the emergence of a bright, glowing, knowing being wave to fully appear at the needed moment. . . .

"We say to you children, listen to the Now as it speaks with a gentle, yet strong, voice to tell of Us. . . . Hear Us come to you in all your moments. See, feel, and know our presence again. Be strong and walk calmly, as we walk beside you—for the Light of ONE glows about you all ways. . . . Thank you for coming, and journey well that you come again."

There was only a vast glow as I listened and watched, and it carried me to my bed and gave me dream stories of sparkling Light. I am aware that I am a wondrous being, lighting my way with love from the hearts of ONE.

CHAPTER 19

Mystical Messages and
Strange Signs in the Sky

Rev. Jayne Howard of Angel Heights, Upperco, Maryland, author of the book *Commune with the Angels*, was in Egypt for fifteen days in 1994 to participate in the opening of the Gateway to Freedom at the Great Pyramid known as 12:12.

On December 12, she was one of a procession of three hundred people who walked holding candles to the Great Pyramid.

"Symbolically, we were bringing our light to the altar of God to honor the Creator and to rededicate ourselves in service to God," Jayne told us. "The members of our group went inside the Great Pyramid, where we remained for most of the early morning hours.

"I was guided by the angels to go first to the King's Chamber."

While in the chamber, Jayne was able to experience the sarcophagus, a large granite coffin that dominates one end of the room. As she lowered herself into the sarcophagus and felt her back touch the granite, "a doorway opened and I found myself in another dimension, standing face-to-face with an angel holding a brilliant torch."

Jayne saw that the torch was in the shape of a lily, with three points blazing—the love, light, and will of God.

"The torch was so many things," Jayne explained, "fire, flower, and Holy Grail cup. The angel handed the torch to me and told me to rise and carry it to the Queen's Chamber."

Jayne went down the steps of the pyramid and walked through a narrow passageway to the Queen's Chamber.

"Even though the chamber was totally dark as I entered the room, I was nearly blinded by the light of the appearance of the Blessed Mother! The Queen of Heaven was in her rightful place—the Queen's Chamber. There she was, the Divine Mother, reminding us that she is always with us inside the Holy of Holies—the altar of God in our hearts."

Jayne was moved to tears by the love that radiated from the Blessed Mother, and she recalled that she kept saying to the angels, "Don't let me forget this, so I may share with others what I am seeing and feeling."

Later, Jayne was inspired by the angels to commission an artist to paint the apparition of the Blessed Mother that she had experienced in the Queen's Chamber on 12:12.

"The angels guided me to meet Marti Betz, and I knew that she was to receive this very special commission," Jayne said. "Together we brought into physical manifestation the heavenly vision of the Divine Mother that I had experienced in Egypt. I knew that it had been a vision to be shared with everyone."

In her opinion, the painting in itself is a message from Mother Mary. "The presence of Mary in the painting is a reflection of the Great Mother that embraces with love our Christ consciousness—the essence of the holy child in each of us.

"The angel in the painting is symbolic of Archangel Raphael, who inspires us to accept our identity as Holy Grail cups and world servers.

"If we let peace begin inside our loving cups–Grail cups, peace will overflow onto Earth. As in the legends of the Holy Grail, the question that needed to be asked prior to experiencing the Grail was, 'Who does the Grail serve?' "

Through the painting of her "Egyptian Encounter of the Divine Kind," Jayne believes that the Great Mother is reminding each of us of the opportunities that we have to serve and to assist in the fulfillment of God's plan for Earth.

The Blessed Mother's Prayers Are Breaking Down Barriers

Dr. Earlyne Chaney, cofounder of Astara, Upland, California, is another well-known mystic who had an activating experience with the Holy Mother in the Great Pyramid.

"Angelic voices sang out, 'Welcome back [to Egypt],' and I was taken through an initiation process by the Great Mother Isis, who became the Blessed Mother Mary," Earlyne told us. "It was given to me at that time that I should conduct a rosary campaign for non-Roman Catholics."

Earlyne firmly believes that it was the Blessed Mother's influence that has been responsible for the resurgence of the spirit of peace in the world.

"Mother Mary has crumbled the Berlin Wall. Remember the Fatima prophecy in which the Blessed Mother promised to convert Russia away from godless communism? Now Gorbachev even visited the pope! Russia may create a new church that will combine the old with the new.

"We know that Soviet scientists made many exciting advances in psychical research," she continued. "They might combine 'psi' with the church and emerge with a new age Christianity that lifts itself away from the old dogmas.

"It is very important in the days to come that we give God alone the credit and the glory. The Blessed Mother's prayers blended with our prayers are breaking down barrier after barrier. We must now see that organized religion strives for a higher level of consciousness."

Suzy Smith, the author of many excellent books on the

paranormal and metaphysics, told us of an experience that completely surprised her one evening in 1984.

"I was in bed, relaxing, sort of meditating but not praying, when suddenly I saw a large eye. As I perceived it, I heard the words in my mind, 'This is the Virgin Mary.'

"I felt a great sense of warmth and love move over me—and I cherished the feeling, as I have since. I've never had any similar occurrence. I've often wondered exactly what it meant."

In a similar encounter, a young woman we'll call Alison, a schoolteacher in the Los Angeles area, told us that she was awakened one night in March 1995 by a greenish, glowing light that soon formed itself into a large eye.

"I reached for the bed lamp, turned it on, and was amazed to see that the large eye was still there. I was not hallucinating. I had not awakened with a bit of dream still stuck in my brain.

"And then as if to prove to me that it was truly real, the large eye slowly blinked at me. That, my friends, gave me a truly eerie sensation.

"I think I would have totally freaked, but it disappeared almost immediately after it had 'winked' at me. And just before it vanished, I heard a soft, musical voice whisper, 'Mary loves you.'

"I have a sister Mary who passed to spirit three years ago. I fell back asleep feeling really good about receiving a message from my deceased sister. I was assured that life continued after death and that Mary still loved me on the Other Side.

"But that morning as I was fixing my breakfast, I received another message very clearly: '*Mother* Mary loves you. You are valued by a source greater than any of your problems.'

"I truly needed to hear that message that morning, as I was having a difficult time at work, feeling as though some of the male teachers had formed a good old boys club that was excluding me and treating me unfairly.

"I felt my confidence being restored, and I knew that I

would now have the necessary and correct energy to handle the situation in a loving but firm manner."

What Can the Stars Tell Us About the Worldwide Appearances of Mother Mary?

Charles Carter Flory of Conifer, Colorado, has a B.A. degree in social science and was employed for a number of years as a social worker and counselor. His true love, however—next to his wife, Lori Jean—is astrology, which he has practiced professionally since 1972.

In the interest of preparing as complete a picture of worldwide Marian manifestations as possible, we asked Charles to look at the matter from an astrological perspective:

According to astrology, the two planets that would rule sightings of Mother Mary would be Neptune and Uranus.

Uranus symbolizes the higher, Divine Mind, and large groups of people, the public. Thus, the mind of the public, the group or mass consciousness.

Neptune symbolizes the higher Divine Love, the Divine Being, the compassionate one. Thus, the love of the Divine Being, the Mother Mary.

Putting the two planets together in their symbology would produce the following: The mind of the public meets the love of the Divine Mother. Why? Because, according to astrology, the world was ready.

From 1906 to 1910, Uranus and Neptune were in opposition exactly eleven times. The Opposition was a very powerful aspect, and for it to occur over eleven times indicates very, very powerful transformative energies—energies that bring opposites together.

During that time Uranus was in the sign of Capricorn. Capricorn is symbolic of a conservative, and perhaps skeptical, public at that time.

Neptune, symbolizing Mother Mary (the Higher Love), was in the sign of Cancer. Cancer signifies the mother. Mary is, of course, commonly known as the Divine Mother, Mother Mary, and our Blessed Mother.

Uranus is the public; Neptune is the Blessed Mother. During the years 1906–1910 the Virgin Mary sightings were welcomed by many believers and scoffed at by many skeptics, as is denoted by this Opposition.

In 1993, Uranus and Neptune were both in Capricorn and were in three conjunction aspects. In this year, Mother Mary (Neptune) and the mass public (Uranus) have met in the same sign. At that time the two planets and the two components—Mother Mary and the mass public—are in agreement and not at odds. The sightings of the Blessed Mother and the blessings that they bring to lead us back to God will be more accepted by the public than ever before.

I do believe that the sightings of Mother Mary have occurred in *all the years* in the twentieth century and in all the years before our century, but the years I have mentioned here—1906–1910 and 1993—had numerous sightings. These were the years that the electromagnetic energies were at a peak, and the sightings of Mary were possible to the greatest number of people.

I would also like to point out that the above-mentioned years were also ones in which the interest in angels by the general public was also very powerful.

The Great Mother and the UFO Mystery

Since the mid-1960s, our investigations into the world of the paranormal and individual mystical experiences have included a great deal of research into the perplexing enigma known as the UFO mystery. To us, the appearance of unidentified objects in our skies and the manifestation of such archetypal images as that of the Great Mother throughout the world signify that we humans are part of a larger community of intelligences, a far more complex hierarchy of powers and principalities, a potentially richer kingdom of beings—both physical and nonphysical—than most of us have been bold enough to believe.

In the highly complex and controversial field of UFO research, there are numerous theories regarding the UFO beings' place of origin and their true identity. Every investigator, regardless of how open-minded he or she strives to be, has a favorite "home base" for the perpetrators of the apparently universal and timeless phenomenon. Most often these arguments are distilled to the central issue of whether the UFO intelligences are physical beings from an extraterrestrial world that have the ability to attain a state of invisibility and to materialize and dematerialize both their bodies and their physical vehicles, or whether the so-called UFOnauts are essentially nonphysical entities from an invisible realm in our own world or from another dimension of reality.

Perhaps both theories are correct. We may be confronted by both kinds of intelligence in our spiritual, intellectual, biological, evolutionary process on planet Earth.

It is not for us to declare a definite link between certain images of Mother Mary and the UFO phenomenon, but there are a number of similarities within the two mysteries that at least demand an open-minded inquiry.

While we believe wholeheartedly in the actual supernatural presence and existence of Mother Mary and the Heavenly Host of attending angels, we have also questioned whether or not in certain instances there is some as yet unknown physical law that could at times activate (or be activated by) our unconscious minds. In some cases, then, the strange things seen from time to time in our planetary skies might be dramatic creations of the human collective unconscious that are sustained by our various belief constructs.

Our good friend, the late Michael Talbot, author of such brilliant and provocative books as *Mysticism and the New Physics*, referred to such phenomena as UFOs and certain appearances of the Virgin Mary, fairies, and so forth, as "protean-psychoid."

They are "protean," he said, because they are all part of the same chameleon-like phenomenon that changes to reflect the belief structures of the time. They are "psychoid" in that they are a paraphysical phenomenon and are related to the psychological state of the observer.

Michael felt that it was the subjective and paraphysical aspect of UFOs and such phenomena that shed the most light on their nature.

In each documented sighting of either UFOs or religious figures, three facts remain:

1. People do experience such phenomena.
2. The various phenomena contain numerous aspects that strongly suggest their physically "real" and objective nature.
3. The various phenomena also contain many elements that strongly suggest their nonphysical, subjective nature.

Michael theorized that the fact that we have not been able to resolve the conflict between the subjective and objective nature of these phenomena may indicate that perhaps the only conflict is in our assumptions concerning such experiences. Perhaps the categories of "real" and "unreal" become meaningless in dealing with phenomena that defy the known scientific laws and principles.

We once asked Michael to set down in essay form his thoughts concerning the dynamics of his theory of "protean-psychoid phenomena," and we herewith excerpt certain thoughts from his provocative observations "beyond real and unreal":

The "perpetrators" of protean-psychoid phenomena reveal many mythological characteristics. The Virgin of Guadalupe, which miraculously appeared upon the tilma of Juan Diego, stands on the horns of a crescent moon, just as Isis was depicted by the ancient Egyptians as standing upon the horns of a crescent.

Many UFO entity encounters, like appearances of the Virgin Mary, have the characteristics of divine revelation. The entity's avowed purpose for appearing to the witness is to convey a sort of heavenly message, or "orgalogue."

Protean-psychoid phenomena have been with us throughout our written history, and most assuredly before. In essence the phenomenon is changeless— the old gods in new clothing.

Although it has been suspected by some investigators that UFOs are carrying on a secret war against humanity and that they are possibly after our life energy, this seems unlikely. The mere fact that the "Trojan horse" of protean-psychoid phenomena appears to have been in our midst for centuries and still hasn't revealed its long-awaited coup d'etat, indicates perhaps that no coup was ever planned.

Whether the Virgin of Fatima is imploring her witnesses to "Pray, pray much and believe in me," or the UFO entity is preaching the cosmic gospel, the message remains the same. Our desire to find meaning in the universe is reflected in the protean-psychoid entities' concern with sustaining our belief.

Protean-psychoid occurrences are filled with archetypal contents. A close study of the phenomenon reveals many "psychological leitmotifs."

For instance, in Tarot iconography the angel Temperance stands with one foot on land and one foot in water. This is interpreted as a metaphoric bridging between the symbol for consciousness (the land), and the symbol for the unconscious (the water).

Interestingly, just as Leonardo da Vinci painted his Madonna and Child with St. Anne, with one foot upon land and one foot upon water, the Virgin of La Salette appeared to the two children Maximin and Melanie with one foot upon the land and one foot upon the water.

The panorama of protean-psychoid phenomena reveals a very subjective quality. A large portion of such encounters are distinctly paraphysical and related to the psychology of humanity in some strange and possibly collective sense. Many orgalogues appear to be evolved by the same psychological motivations that create both myth and religion.

However, these phenomena also reveal a physical and objective aspect. UFOs can be tracked on radar; the Virgin Mary can give her witnesses real roses; UFOs and their occupants leave footprints and burnt circles in deserted fields.

As I have just shown, the objective explanation for these phenomena do not explain their paraphysical nature. Similarly, the folie à deux, or shared hallucination, simply does not explain their physical nature. A new view of the phenomena must take both aspects into account.

Humanity's emotional need for a cohesive mythic structure, in one sense, generates the various phenomena. We are creating them on a collective level in much the same way that we create dreams on an individual level.

The belief that *we* generate such phenomena still entails the categories of real and unreal. In dealing with omnijectivity, the belief that reality is plastic or ideational must necessarily transcend this notion as well.

In considering these phenomena with the idea that we generate them, it is implicit that *we* are somehow more real than the phenomena. The myth that we generate protean-psychoid phenomena is only temporarily efficacious. Beyond this myth, beyond real and unreal, lies an absolute elsewhere that is presently being "realized" by the two branches of science most concerned with consciousness and reality. In the study of human behavior and quantum mechanics, three new views are materializing that will radically affect our position and role in the universe.

These are:

1. Consciousness and reality are a continuum.
2. Such phenomena as UFOs are part of our "self-reference cosmology."
3. All possible realities "exist" in an indefinite number of universes.

The myth that these phenomena *are generating us* is most assuredly just as valid.

When seventy thousand people witness the miracle of the sun at Fatima, we can greet it as an omnijective occurrence. The faith of seventy thousand anxious spectators is surely as potent as the faith of the Vajrayana yogin who does not believe in a metaphysical hierarchy and yet calls forth its deities.

However, to believe that the seventy thousand spectators are somehow more "real" than the Virgin of Fatima is again simply an efficacious myth. Somewhere, some*when*, there is probably a Virgin of Fatima who believes that she generated the seventy thousand followers!

Every consciousness can function as if reality is generated by it because there are an indefinite number of self-reference cosmologies. Protean-psychoid phenomena are simply a type of self-reference cosmology. . . . Undoubtedly, there are no limits to the omnijective nature of reality.

Thomas Mann states: "As in a dream it is *our own will* that unconsciously appears as inexorable objective destiny, everything in it proceeding out of ourselves and each of us being the secret theatre manager of our own dreams. So also in reality the great dream which a single essence, the will itself, dreams with us all, *our fate may be the product of our inmost selves*, of our wills; and we are actually *bringing about* what seems to be happening to us.

We know that "something extraordinary" has been taking place on this planet for at least the past two thousand years and that in the past fifty or so years, the mysterious signs and images that have been manifesting in our skies have been accelerating in their interaction with us. Whether the entities associated with these manifestations have appeared as angels or Mother Mary or cosmic teachers, they seem to be preparing us for a fast-approaching time of transition and transformation on Mother Earth. This period, we have been told, will be a difficult one, and for generations various prophets and revelators have been referring to it as the Great Cleansing, Judgment Day, or Armageddon.

Although these beings appear willing to guide us by their example and profess to love us with all their spiritual essence, none of them have ever promised an easy deliverance from our ecological, sociological, biological, ethical or moral sins. An essential element of the messages that issue from Mother Mary and the various angelic or "protean-psychoid" entities is that we as individuals and as a species must somehow learn to manage our own affairs so that we may achieve a clearer understanding of our true role in the cosmic scheme of things and attain a level of awareness whereby we attain a state of oneness and self-sufficiency that acknowledges the god spark within each of us.

CHAPTER 20

Mother Mary, Pray for Us at the Hour of Our Death

In our files we have numerous accounts of devout men, women, and children who saw or heard profound evidence of the Blessed Mother and her angels ministering to the dying as they stood vigil at the deathbeds of family and friends. Here are only a few of the moving, inspirational stories.

Mother Mary and Two Magnificent Angels Appeared to Take His Wife Home to Heaven

Philip Buckholz of Dearborn, Michigan, saw Mother Mary and two "magnificent" angels appear in his wife's hospital room shortly after she died.

"Signe had opened her eyes briefly," Philip said. "She had been sleeping for two or three hours. I lost track of time as I dozed in the chair beside her bed. She smiled at me, and I took her hand.

"She closed her eyes again, and something made me turn to look over my shoulder. There I clearly saw the Blessed Virgin and two tall, magnificent angels, one on either side of her.

"An inner knowing told me to get the priest to administer the sacraments. He had looked in on Signe only a few minutes before, and since she was sleeping, he had continued his visitations to others farther along the corridor.

"When I returned with the priest to Signe's room, the Blessed Mother and the angels were no longer there. I knew that they had taken Signe's soul with them. A doctor soon confirmed that my wife had died peacefully while she slept."

Mother Mary Allowed Her to Visit Heaven with Her Dying Son

Vera Krein of Pittsburgh saw an image of Mother Mary in the sickroom of her teenage son three hours before his death. It was Mary, she said later, who had called Alan out of his body.

"I had been taking turns with my husband maintaining a bedside vigil," Vera said. "About two o'clock in the morning, Alan suddenly tried to sit up. His eyes opened wide in wonder, and he pointed toward a corner of the room.

" 'Look, Mom,' he said excitedly. 'It's the Blessed Mother.'

"At first I saw nothing, but I began to say the rosary," Vera said. "At Alan's insistence, I kept my eyes on the corner of the room where he was certain that he had seen Mother Mary.

"And then I saw her! She was wearing a white veil and wore a sky blue, flowing dress."

The next instant, Vera Krein stated later, she seemed to lose consciousness, and she has only a dim memory of slumping back in the chair at Alan's bedside.

"For three hours I was with Alan and the Blessed Mother in a beautiful paradise," she said. "It was as if she was showing him how lovely his existence would be in Heaven. And, although it made me weep, I think it was her tranquil mother energy that helped Alan to accept his death. She would be his Holy Mother in Heaven, as I had been privileged to be his earthly mother.

"We saw many angels who projected such love and warmth toward Alan and me.

"One of them told me that it was not usual for a relative or friend of one about to die to be able to view Heaven together with the dear one, but they wished to ease the sorrow in my heart and to provide me with some comfort before Alan's passing. They knew that I had always been a mother who so loved my son. Mother Mary said that she knew how painful it was to lose a son.

"Finally, the Holy Mother said that I must return to my physical body. Alan's soul must stay there with her and the angels. I was able to give my son one last embrace, and then two stately angels appeared, one on each side of me, and brought me back to the hospital room.

"When I awakened, it was five o'clock. I had been out of my body with Alan and the Holy Mother in heaven for three hours.

"I touched my son's body, and I knew that Alan was dead before the doctor confirmed it. With tears of sorrow and of gratitude, I thanked Mother Mary for allowing me to be with him for a time in the spirit world."

A Doctor Saw a "Beautiful Lady in White" Embrace a Dying Boy's Soul

Dr. Erwin Stallings, a retired general practitioner from North Dakota, said that he would never forget the time that he was visiting a sick child who had been slowly dying from the ravages of typhoid fever.

"In those days, back in the late 1920s, I'm afraid that the Roman Catholics and the Protestants in the area still had their little feuds, some serious and some just good-natured teasing that could turn sour if one or the other pushed it too far.

"This little boy that I was tending was the youngest child of a hardworking German Catholic family. Since I was a staunch Methodist, we had exchanged some salty words in our day, but when one of their four kids was sick, it didn't matter to them if I worshipped cows or trees. They wanted me there looking after their children."

Late one afternoon in August, just after Dr. Stallings had finished examining the boy, he heard a rustling sound off to his right side.

"I figure that I was hearing the sound of the mother's dress, so without turning around, I expressed my sad regret that I didn't think there was anything more that I could do for the lad. His condition had not improved, and it seemed to be quickly worsening. I suggested that they call their priest for last rites. My pills and powders could not help him any longer.

"When there was no response, I turned to see a beautiful lady dressed in white standing just a few inches from my right shoulder. She seemed not to pay any attention to me, but she approached the boy in his bed. I knew that she was not any member of the family.

"The lovely woman bent over the child, then took the spirit form of the little boy into her arms.

"I was so stunned by the action that I thought my knees would buckle. I was witnessing a sight that few mortals are privileged to see.

"And what I next beheld was even more startling. The beautiful lady passed right through the wall with the child's spirit in her arms.

"I sat quietly in a chair for several minutes as I sought to recover my mental balance.

"When my wits had returned and I could examine the boy, I verified what I already knew. He had died at the moment when the beautiful woman in white had lifted his soul from his body.

"A few minutes later, I told his weeping parents that

their youngest child had died, but I could offer my earnest conviction that I had seen Mother Mary herself carry his soul off to Heaven. Although I was Methodist born and bred, I had always been taught to respect the Mother of Jesus. And the beautiful woman in white had looked just like some of the statues of Mary that I had seen in Catholic churches."

The Blessed Mother Told Her in a Dream That Her Sister Was Dying

LaVerne Delaney of Albany, New York, told of a dream that she'd had in which an image of Mother Mary informed her that her older sister Ginger was dying.

"Whether it's a dark Irish curse or a blessing," LaVerne said, "I had experienced a similar dream before the death of our mother, my cousin Peter, and a close school friend. Because of such a sorrowful track record, I knew that I had better pay attention to this sad dream about Ginger."

LaVerne was already packing for the trip to Vermont when a telegram arrived that confirmed her dream vision of Ginger's approaching death. She and her husband, Pat, left immediately to be at her sister's bedside.

"When we arrived in her hospital room, Ginger's eyes were closed, but she seemed to be aware that we were at her side," LaVerne said.

As she bent to kiss her cheek, Ginger spoke in a barely audible whisper. "Did you have another of your dreams, sis?"

LaVerne told her that she had received a dream vision of her condition.

"Then you shouldn't be sad, little sister, for you know that Mother Mary will come for me soon," Ginger said with a weak smile. "But I am so glad that you and Pat came all this way to say good-bye to me."

Pat suggested that they say the rosary and pray together.

Suddenly Ginger's eyes opened. "Oh, my goodness, sis.

You and Pat got here just in time. There's an angel at the window right now."

Both Pat, who was standing in front of the window, and LaVerne turned to see for themselves.

"Oh, Pat," Ginger whispered, "you're blocking the pathway. Please step aside."

Pat did as his sister-in-law requested; then heeding an intuitive flash, he left the room to get a doctor or a nurse.

"She's here," Ginger smiled. "Behind the angel I can see Mother Mary beckoning to me. And, oh, honey, there is Mom . . . and Pop, too. I guess . . . it's time for me to go home. I love you. . . ."

Pat and a doctor entered the room at the same moment that a sudden wind suddenly stirred the curtains—and the breath of life left Ginger's body.

"My dear sister's face bore a lovely and restful smile as her soul left with her guardian angel and Mother Mary," LaVerne Delaney said.

CHAPTER 21

Multicolored Rain at Sabana Grande, Puerto Rico

Dona Nora Freise sat before the spring near Rincon de Sabana Grande, Puerto Rico, in the wheelchair that had carried her helpless body for forty-seven years and wondered about what the three children had been saying. Juan Angel Collado and his two friends, the sisters Ramonita and Isidra Belen, had been telling everyone that they had seen the Holy Mother in the small spring under some mango trees.

Could it be true? Had the children truly seen the Blessed Mother on the way home from their elementary school that day in April 1953?

Dona Nora had been a paraplegic for more than four decades. Was she being foolish in hoping that Mother Mary truly had appeared at the spring and had blessed its water with healing energy?

At first nearly all the people of Rincon de Sabana Grande had either scolded the children or laughed at them for having told such a foolish story. But Dona Nora knew that the three little ones stubbornly held fast to their account of having seen the Blessed Mother at the spring.

Juan, Ramonita, and Isidra never changed their story. They never added more details to make it more incredible.

They never retracted any aspects to make it more believable.

Soon people began to wonder. Perhaps the children were telling the truth.

More and more men and women had begun to come to the spring and its tiny stream to see for themselves if Mary would appear to them. But only the three children had been able to see the Holy Mother and speak to her.

Dona Nora Freise believed that many times throughout the history of religious enlightenment and revelation, children had been given an ability to see angels and holy figures that adults were sometimes denied. In her heart she believed that Juan, Ramonita, and Isidra had truly seen Mother Mary just as they said they had.

She dipped a bottle into the stream and took some of the spring water home with her to Mayaguez. She would drink of the holy water—and she would be healed!

A few days later, to the utter amazement of her family and friends, the woman who had been a paraplegic for forty-seven years was able to stand. Within another day or two, she was able to walk and permanently abandon her wheelchair.

The miraculous healing of Dona Nora inspired dozens of others to fill their own bottles, jugs, and pitchers from the spring. Crowds of pilgrims began to stream into the area.

Then the three children revealed that the Blessed Mother had told them that she would perform a miracle at 11:00 A.M. on May 25—a month and two days after she had first manifested to them.

As word spread of the impending miracle promised by Mother Mary, huge crowds began to make their way to the spring. Because there were no serviceable roads that led to the stream and clump of mango trees, people were forced to walk a considerable distance to the appointed area.

Hundreds arrived on May 24 and slept overnight on the ground, spreading their bedrolls as near to the sacred site as possible. Priests and politicians lay next to journalists and attorneys—all come to see for themselves if the Blessed Mother would appear. Enveloping the entire area were the sick, the halt, and the lame—all hoping for their own personal miracle.

By mid-morning on May 25, it was scorching hot. A brilliant sun ruled supreme over a cloudless sky.

And then at exactly eleven o'clock it began to rain.

While some of those pilgrims clustered at the spring that morning might have thought the sudden manifestation of rain out of a sizzling, cloudless sky was miracle enough, Mother Mary had an even more impressive display of holy might in mind. The rain was multicolored, and the assembled multitude was soon being bathed in drops of water of every hue in the rainbow.

One of the pilgrims who received a miracle healing that day was Paula Carrasco of Miami, Florida, who had suffered for many years from a chronic neck ailment. Paula had been fitted with a metallic orthopedic brace that began at her waist, covered her chest, and ended at her jaw. It was, she said, like wearing a metal cage.

Specialists had advised her that there was not a doctor in the world who could heal her, and her husband, Felix Carrasco, had taken her to Puerto Rico only for a change of scene. Neither of them had heard a word about the three children and the Blessed Mother of Sabana Grande.

As destiny would have it, they arrived in San Juan just as all Puerto Rico was talking about the excitement that was to take place at Sabana Grande in a few days. At the same time, of course, they heard about the miraculous healing of Dona Nora.

Felix and Paula resolved to travel to Sabana Grande so that she might present herself to the Holy Mother for healing.

But when they arrived on the evening of May 24, Paula was so depressed at the sight of the thousands of men and women lined up for an opportunity to be healed at the spring that she fainted.

When she regained consciousness, she was taken to the

local health center at Sabana Grande. The attending physician advised her to rest, and she slept for a few hours in the special chair that she had brought with her. Ever since the orthopedic surgeons had fitted her with the torturous brace, it had been impossible for her to sleep in a bed.

At 4:00 A.M., Paula rose and began to make her way to the elementary school. Although it was extremely difficult for her to walk, she was determined somehow to reach the stream. Four national guard members took pity on her struggles and carried her nearer to the overflow of the spring that was now known as the Stream of the Virgin Mary.

Later, as the miracle rain descended, Paula said that she saw many wonderful images, such as the Sacred Heart of Jesus and many flowers that seemed to float in the air.

Then she saw a nun standing near her. "Come forward, child, take my hand," the sister told her.

"Somehow this nun just stood out in the crowd," Paula said. "I was surrounded by thousands of people, yet all I seemed to be able to focus on was this beautiful, smiling nun. I wanted so badly to take her hand as she had asked me."

The nun suddenly opened her arms and turned in all directions.

"I now understood that no one else in the vast crowd could see the nun," Paula said. "I then realized that I was beholding the Blessed Mother rather than a nun."

At the very moment of her realization, Paula felt an electrical jolt in her head. She had no explanation for the painful shock, but she now felt that it was no longer important whether or not she would be healed. The satisfaction of seeing the Blessed Mother was enough for her.

Paula saw Juan, Ramonita, and Isidra pointing at her. The crowd was so thick around the children that she could not hear what they were saying, but it seemed to her that they wished to approach her.

At last a man came and told her that the children were passing the word forward that Mother Mary wished someone to remove her braces. Paula was already aware that she could move her neck, so she offered no resistance when two men removed the oppressive braces.

"I was able to hold my head high," she said. "I was able to turn it. And I could walk without help from anyone."

As Paula turned to walk away from the stream, people all around her began to shout and cheer that she had been healed.

When Paula and Felix returned to Miami and went to the specialists who had predicted that she would have to spend her life in a painfully uncomfortable brace, the doctors could hardly believe that they were examining the same woman.

After her miracle cure Paula converted to Catholicism, and on each May 25 for many years to come she returned to Sabana Grande and the Stream of the Virgin to honor the Blessed Mother and give thanks.

CHAPTER 22

Life's Pathway and the Mother Mary Energy

In September 1995, we received a newsletter entitled "Life's Pathway—Angel Whispers," on which one of our readers had written: "As you can see from the attached, the Holy Mother has truly appeared at Life's Pathway on a regular basis."

With such an intriguing recommendation, we immediately contacted Rev. Pam Wade and Rev. Marie Trump, who proved to be most cooperative in providing us with a number of inspirational details of their work at Life's Pathway, an educational-spiritual retreat located in the country outside of Leavenworth, Indiana.

Rev. Pam has no idea why she should be the one chosen to share the words of Mother Mary to others. "There's nothing glamorous or outstanding about me," she protested. "I'm no different or any more special than anyone else—and by no means am I as deserving of this honor as many others I know. But for some reason it happened, and for some reason I have been allowed to be an instrument for the message of love that she shares. I won't question God. All I want is to be allowed to serve in the best manner I am capable. My favorite song growing up in church was, 'Just as I Am.' I guess that is all that I can offer."

Life's Pathway is located on twenty-two acres nestled in the gently rolling hills of southern Indiana. Seven years ago, Rev. Marie Trump founded the organization to serve as a nondenominational church and school that would emphasize metaphysical teachings.

On September 23, 1994, Rev. Pam Wade suddenly found herself being employed as the host for the teachings of Mary, the Mother of Jesus.

When she asked why, Mary answered:

"Workers of the Light, you have called. If you choose a different name with which to identify this energy, other than what has been identified as 'Mary,' you may choose to identify it as the 'Lady of Light.' The name is not important. The energy will remain the same.

"Many will ask, 'Why here? Why this place, this organization, these people?' 'Why would information through one who serves as a threshold for humankind to uplift itself be offered here, now, in this manner?'

"The information is offered here because there are open hearts here. There are those who seek to serve the Light. There are those who have made commitments within their hearts to be one with the energy and the path of my Son. . . .

"This is a place of oneness, which works for the unification of humankind. The people here have come together to serve as instruments for awakening the hearts of humankind.

"Why now? Because it is time! Humankind is ready. You have offered this place as a vehicle, and you have given it to God—and it will be used. It is being aligned with 'home,' and in that alignment the energy of miracles will begin. . . .

"In your receiving, awaken, and allow your illumination to shine forth. Amen."

The above is a portion of the first public message that Mary, the Lady of Light, offered through the agency of Rev. Pam Wade for a gathering at Life's Pathway. But according to Rev. Marie Trump, the founder of the organization, the presence of Mary, Mother of Jesus, began earlier in a most dramatic manner.

"Several years ago, my son and his wife gave me a beautiful bust of Mother Mary with the Child Jesus," Rev. Marie explained. "Since I am not Catholic, I didn't say the rosary, but I did find myself talking to Mary at times. I would especially ask for help when I was worried about one of my children—and it always seemed that help came."

When she founded Life's Pathway in 1988, Rev. Marie felt guided to take her Mary statue with her and to place it on a special healing table in the sanctuary. She felt that the bust would be an appropriate complement to the healing service that was always included as a regular part of the Sunday service.

About a year later, Life's Pathway was able to move into a larger building. "We poured our love and energy into fixing the place up," Rev. Marie remembered, "and once again our healing services became the focal point of our Sunday observance, with the Mary bust prominently displayed."

Soon after the acquisition of the new building, Rev. Pam Wade began a weekly session of channeling information from a being who identified itself as "Mikiah." The sessions were conducted in a large room next to the sanctuary, and one evening all those in attendance became very excited when they discovered that the mantle on Mary's bust was turning blue.

"I wondered if someone was putting blue paint on it, and I wasn't very pleased about it," Rev. Marie said. "If it was some kind of hoax, I would not let it go too far. I don't believe in fakery, and I certainly didn't want Life's Pathway to get this type of reputation. Some people had a camera in their car, so they took some pictures to document the alleged event."

The following week, additional photographs were taken, and Rev. Marie was taken aback when the second set of pictures revealed that Mary's head had turned. "In the first set of photographs Mary was looking out over the baby's head. In the second she bent her head toward the baby's head and was almost able to kiss him."

Whether or not someone had applied some blue paint to the bust, the second set of pictures proved that something was going on. No human hand could have turned the head without breaking it.

Rev. Marie decided that Mary wanted something from Life's Pathway, and during her next "chat" with the Blessed Mother she thanked her for the many times she had helped her get through a problem. She also told Mother Mary that if she should need any help from her human agency, would she please let her know and guide her to do the right thing at the right time.

"I feel very blessed that the Mother Mary energy has chosen Life's Pathway to work through," Rev. Marie said. "And I pray that we can get her messages out to those who need the loving help that she is offering."

Mary speaks on October 19, 1995:

"You, as workers of the Light, offer to humanity the opportunity to establish a foundation of change. This foundation of change begins within your heart and spreads forth. You offer to humankind a new word: unity. You offer to humankind a new understanding of peace. For as people find peace upon Earth, they fear the change that it brings about.

"If there was true peace on Earth, there would be no need for the establishments. There would be no need for the controls. There would be no need, as was shared by my Son, for the requirement for ten rules or laws or commandments. Each man would do and say and be what is best for all, for the one commandment that He offered would fulfill within all people the unity to love one another. In that loving is found respect, concern, and caring. In that loving is found forgiveness. For in that loving is found the heart of God."

The Experience of Rev. Janet Missi

The onset of the Mary energy to Rev. Janet Missi came in the summer of 1994 when Rev. Pam Wade was channeling Mikiah:

"She told us a new energy was wanting to present some information to us in a different way. I know that Pam went through a lot of self-examination before she allowed this to happen to her. She questioned her worthiness, and she wondered how this new energy would affect her personally. And, of course, she questioned how this would affect Life's Pathway, as well as her family and her community. Pam has always been a perfect example of service to humanity, so with reluctance she agreed to be a vehicle for the sharing of energy and information."

Rev. Janet said that the group knew from the Mikiah information that the Mary energy would manifest publicly at their September 1994 gathering. "Mary has never talked personally with any one person. She has given only universal information or guidance for our church. She has, though, given us personal information on a universal level with which we can identify individually."

Mary speaks in October 1994:

"Your Earth is full of words that fall upon ears which do not hear. Your Earth is full of nonproduction.

"You, as workers of the light of truth and love, are the instruments of growth and enlightenment upon the Earth. Your hearts and minds are in the unity of creation. Your hearts and your souls cry out to put away falsity. And as you bring forth that message upon the Earth, you shine forth in love. And in that love, humankind sees possibilities.

"As your structures change in the coming year, you will find many things changing that have had many years of establishment. Your governments, your religions, will be found to be standing on ground that is not solid. You will find many things to be brought into light. You will find changes that reflect fear within the hearts of many men.

"Let not your hearts be troubled. You know within your being that the Father has a purpose and a path for creation. It is not haphazard. It is not one of chance. Your soul is a part of that purpose. And in this time upon your Earth, your soul is awakening to that which it has known.

"Those who stand in power at this time will falter. . . . Those who stand in power in your churches will be changing very quickly.

"As the eyes of man seek truth and the heart of man cries out—and as you enter into a time of confusion upon your Earth during this season of silence—you can seek within yourself the love and the alignment with the heart of God. And you may maintain your strength through such alignment.

"As has been said, 'Seek ye first the kingdom.' And wherein lies the kingdom? The Kingdom of Heaven is within. Seek ye first that peace so that you may share it with others. Your lives are changing—and the changes that you have experienced as individuals will now come forth to all humankind."

A Series of Miracles as Witnessed by Kathleen Abrams

According to Kathleen Abrams, this is a condensed version of the many miracles that were wrought by Mother Mary on May 19, 20, and 21, 1995, and were witnessed by about thirty-five people "who opened their hearts and surrendered their beliefs to a higher power.

"Many of the miracles were recorded on video, Polaroid film, and various cameras belonging to the witnesses," Kathleen Abrams stated. "I personally used five rolls of film, taking before, during, and after shots of the grounds and the sky above us."

At the beginning of the gathering, Mother Mary announced that "the doors will be flung aside. All of Heaven and Earth have the opportunity to share in the energy of the universe. No barriers exist."

Kathleen Abrams said that she witnessed a visual manifestation of Mother Mary as the left hand of the statue of Mary in the grotto was raised twice in succession in a wave of "hello."

According to Kathleen: "The statue actually moved, and it was startling!"

On Friday, May 19, at 10:30 P.M., Mother Mary, speaking through Rev. Pam Wade, called for a pitcher of tap water and instructed Rev. Janet Missi to go into the kitchen for a large bowl.

"When Janet returned to the sanctuary with a large crystal bowl," Kathleen said, "Mary asked her to pour the tap water in the clear bowl. As she did this, the water turned into a white, bubbly substance. The magnificent and intense fragrance of roses filled the room and permeated the oily water. Mary then immersed Pam's hands in the oil and anointed her forehead with the sign of the cross. Mary then asked Janet to pass the fragrant water throughout the room, with each person anointing the forehead of the person sitting next to them."

On Saturday, May 20, at 6:30 P.M., out in the Mary Grotto, Mary spoke world messages after saying the rosary.

"During this session," Kathleen Abrams said, "we were asked to 'breathe the breath of God.' At that moment the intense smell of roses flowed over all the people gathered in the Mary Grotto. All could smell the aroma, even though there were no roses present on the grounds at that time. The fragrance lasted for over an hour, and many people continued to catch waves of the scent throughout the evening and even the next morning."

During that same session Mary instructed those assembled to "look upon the face of God."

"We had a video camera going, as well as several other cameras," Kathleen said. "We immediately got a Polaroid picture of what is known as the 'Doorway to Heaven.' It is a magnificent photo of a phenomenon that has taken place at many of the Mary apparitions around the world.

"A second Polaroid was taken immediately following the first, and we saw that it revealed a huge pillar of gold light descending down from Heaven to where we were all standing."

Next, according to Kathleen's account, the eyes on the statue of Mary in the grotto opened.

"This was recorded on my before and after photographs," she stated. "Normally, the eyes on the statue are almost nonexistent, appearing almost closed. My photos clearly show that the eyes of the statue of Mary opened, then closed again."

The video camera captured the face of Christ beginning to form over Rev. Pam's face.

"Also visible to many—and the camera—were the shapes of a diamond and a cross on her forehead.

"We were asked to release our fears as changes come forth on Earth. We were told to pray unceasingly and to maintain our focus so that our illumination would shine forth. Mary always closes a session with the words: 'In your receiving, awaken, and allow your illumination to shine forth.' "

During that same May weekend, Kathleen Abrams said that another miracle occurred when Mary requested that all those present on the grounds form a healing circle and sing, "I am a circle; I am healing you. You are a circle; you are healing me. Unite us. Be one."

"At this time Mary, utilizing Rev. Pam's physical being, approached the circle and walked around us, looking straight at each person in succession," Kathleen said. "As I caught her eye, she walked up to a large crystal bowl filled with water that was placed in the circle. Standing between two members of the circle, she placed open hands above the bowl, then inside the water.

"Simultaneously with this movement, what sounded like hundreds of stones flowed out of her open palms into the bowl.

"This she did twice, allowing anyone to approach her who wished to see the stones flow out of her palms—now positioned about four inches above the rim of the bowl. The fragrance of roses was again very strong.

"Everyone was allowed to take as many of the stones as they wanted. Stones of different colors continued to appear as people took them out of the bowl. They were small in size, and yet it sounded as though hundreds had fallen out of the open palms of Rev. Pam's hands to hit the clear crystal bowl quite noisily.

"This was an overwhelming miracle for me," Kathleen stated. "To see Mary placing Pam's open palms over the clear bowl and to witness hundreds of gemstones falling out of her hands was an incredible experience. Mother Mary told us that the stones were a reminder never to allow fear to stand between us and the Father—and to remember always the promise of love.

"The grounds at Life's Pathway are truly sacred, and I would like to encourage anyone to go there and to witness for themselves the spiritual and physical miracles occurring there on every third Saturday of the month," Kathleen Abrams said, concluding her account for us. "I have felt especially blessed to be a part of this place. Mary promised that she will be present there for at least the next three years."

Mary speaks on September 15, 1995:

"You who gather here . . . are set upon a task of opening the awareness of humankind. . . . The words that we have to share cannot be understood by those who would try to perceive, analyze, or dissect, for the information that we give is presented to your heart.

"If you walk in doubt, if you walk in hesitation, you serve a God of fear. This is not the desire of the Creator. This is not the information brought by my Son upon this Earth. . . . Do not fear the energy of change, for fear stands between you and completeness.

"Do not be alarmed if your perception is not clear. You must see through your heart, for reason will not be found.

"You have called, and we have come. In your requesting our presence, we come to fulfill a promise that has been made upon your Earth . . . a promise that you are never alone . . . a promise that is fulfilled within your being through the presence of love."

The Testimony of Sharon Yashsoda Freeman

A Pathway of Change

Sharon Yashsoda Freeman said that her first introduction to Life's Pathway and the Mother Mary energy was in September 1994, when a longtime friend who was living in Indiana invited her to come and experience what she called "a new level of spiritual awakening."

Sharon was both excited and intrigued by her friend's words. "I trusted her very much," she said. "She has been the catalyst for many of my spirit-seeking journeys over the past eighteen years. I knew if this place resonated so deeply with her, I was certainly going to explore the possibilities for myself. At that time I had no way of knowing where this exploration would lead me."

At the time of her friend's invitation, Sharon was still living in California. While she was planning her trip to Indiana for the weekend retreat, she became aware of a deep inner prompting to move from California back to her home state of Florida. The motion for complete life changes was already beginning.

Her friend had given her a great deal to think about during the weeks before she arrived in Indiana. The experiences that she had shared with Sharon about recent sessions with Mother Mary had increased her motivation and her growing sensation of excitement "to a point of frenzy."

Finally, on September 22, 1994, she was there.

"My first impression of Life's Pathway was of a small, charming community of people whose warm and accepting energy captured my heart immediately," Sharon said. "I *knew* these people from a place deep inside me that could not be denied. In some strange, mystical way I had come home."

The Friday workshop began early in the day so those gathered could create the energy for a loving connection between them. They prayed together, sang together, and ate together.

"In our joining and blending of the tremendous energy of this place, a bond of love and light began to flow. I was walking on clouds most of the day. That evening we gathered to hear the weekend's first session with Mother Mary through the agency of Rev. Pam Wade."

Sharon said Mary's words were of an energy that held her fast in her seat. "I felt my heart open with love, and I could only sit and wonder at the presence of such an energy. I heard her call us 'workers of the Light,' and my joy knew no bounds. I had often thought of myself as a worker of the Light, but no one had ever referred to me in those terms. I was moved beyond any other experience that I had ever known by the soft, gentle voice and the love emanating in the room."

There were two sessions on Saturday, September 25. During the daytime gathering, Mother Mary manifested many mother-of-pearl and garnet stones to be given to all of those present.

For the evening session Sharon saw to it that she was sitting "right up front in the first row." The utterances from Mother Mary moved her "beyond the words to a place inside that I had never consciously experienced before. The person that I had been when I arrived at Life's Pathway seemed to disappear."

When the session ended, Sharon knew she was in the room, but she found herself unable to move or to make a sound. "People were coming up and speaking to me. I heard their words, but I could not respond. Something inside me had been touched and was now a part of my being. I needed time to assimilate all of this. I stayed in a frozen state for about twenty minutes. Tears ran profusely down my face. I had discovered something within myself that I had not known existed—and I would never be the same person I was before."

During the Sunday session, Mother Mary came forth into the group, anointed each person individually, and gave each of them a private message. She told Sharon that she was walking a path of change and that she would become a clear channel for love.

"I left Indiana and Life's Pathway on Monday, September 27, my birthday," Sharon said. "For the first time I knew that I had a purpose in life. I did not concern myself at that time with the need to know what the purpose was. I believed that when I was ready, God would reveal the purpose to me."

Sharon returned to her home state of Florida. As Mother Mary had indicated, she underwent tremendous life-changing experiences, which included entering a treatment program for her seventeen-year addiction to marijuana. She returned to Life's Pathway a year later.

"I arrived just in time for the anniversary of my previous Mother Mary gathering," Sharon said. "I slept in a tent on the grounds and worked in preparation for the event. Once again I was uplifted and inspired by the messages given. I felt certain that while I didn't know how things would unfold, I was indeed in the right place.

"As I look back over the past year, I accept fully that my encounter with Life's Pathway and the glorious Mother Mary energy of love and light I received created the catalyst for the many life changes that have occurred to me on my path as a worker of the Light."

Awaken—and Allow Your Illumination to Shine Forth

Rev. Pam Wade told us that, like so many others, Sharon Yashsoda Freeman experienced a healing energy in the presence of Mother Mary. Such remarkable encounters are being compiled, together with Mother Mary's words, into book form so that "many may hear and no longer allow fear to stand as an obstacle in their path to God."

Mary speaks on September 15, 1995:

"Let it not be said of you that your light shone in

darkness and that the darkness could not comprehend. Let it be said of you that this is a person that seeks for love, for truth, for understanding, for oneness, and for blending with the All.

"As your light begins to shine forth more strongly, your world will change around and about you. You may find that those situations within your existence can no longer be tolerated without love and light within them. And as they realign, a brightness will come forth.

"We will be at this place for as long as it continues to shine forth its light and has need of us.

"You have within your group those who have agreed and who have made an alignment of their soul with the truth that comes forth from this place with the healing that it offers. Our energy will be here for that.

"In your receiving, awaken, and allow your illumination to shine forth. Amen."

AFTERWORD

Allow the Divine Mother to Enter Your Life

When Sherry Hansen Steiger was about eleven years old and residing with her parents in Mankato, Minnesota, she had an encounter with Mother Mary that grew out of a very frightening experience.

Both of her parents had gone to the grocery store, and Sherry and a girlfriend were home alone. Glancing out the kitchen window, Sherry noticed that the sky had turned blood red as the day approached sunset. Then as the two girls watched, the sun appeared to be moving, spinning, dancing in the sky.

Sherry remembers that she and her friend became convinced that the world was ending. Her parents were somewhere shopping, and Doomsday would arrive while she was alone home with her girlfriend.

"Silly as it may seem now, we hid under the kitchen table, desperate to survive somehow the end of the world," Sherry said. "It was as we clung to each other under the table that something almost as frightening as the dancing sun occurred. A brilliant light appeared in the kitchen, a light that soon transformed into the image of a beautiful lady dressed in white."

Sherry clearly remembers the lady calming the two girls and telling them not to be afraid. "She also spoke quite a bit about prophecy and a number of future events that would occur, but I have no clear memory of precisely what she said. Just bits and pieces that sometime come back to me even now as an adult."

A few years later when Sherry's family moved to Grosse Pointe, Michigan, one of her best friends was a Roman Catholic who invited her to attend Mass. "It was there that I, who came from an Evangelical United Brethren religious background, first saw a life-size statue of the Blessed Mother. I was astonished to see that this representation of Mother Mary closely resembled the beautiful lady who had appeared in our kitchen in Mankato."

As she learned more about the significance of Mother Mary in the lives of her Catholic friends, Sherry began to reassess an experience that had occurred to her as she attended summer camp in upper Michigan when she was seven years old.

It was a hot, humid night. All the girls were bedded down in their bunks, and the lights were out. Sherry had just finished her bedtime prayers when she thought someone had turned on the brightest light she had ever seen.

In a corner of the room, at ceiling level, she saw a stream of bluish-white light take on the shape of the most beautiful, gentle, and loving woman that she had ever seen. The lady seemed to come through the ceiling, and a brilliant illumination surrounded her as she hovered with outstretched arms and spoke to Sherry.

The lady delivered a clear message for Sherry and for all the girls present. She told them just how very special they each were and how very much God loved them.

Sherry remembered clearly how all the girls in the cabin were on their knees in prayerlike positions. Yet from time to time they seemed to glance toward Sherry as if they were somehow expecting her to act as a kind of intermediary for them with the heavenly being.

Later, after the beautiful lady had disappeared, Sherry had tears streaming from her eyes when she tried to explain the "disturbance" in the cabin to the camp counselors.

Looking around at her cabin mates, she saw that many of the other girls were crying as well.

Some of the girls testified that they, too, had witnessed the coming and going of the illuminated being and saw and heard her speaking to Sherry. Others said that a brilliant light had awakened them, and then they heard Sherry carrying on a conversation with the heavenly visitor.

"In retrospect, from that day forward, it seemed as if a plan had been set in motion for my life pathway," Sherry commented.

"I had been infused with some sort of an understanding of the sacredness and connectedness of all of God's creatures. A life pattern had been established that would guide and direct me in difficult times ahead and sustain me with a sense of mission and purpose."

Although Sherry would one day become a Protestant minister, the image of the Blessed Mother has always been of vital importance to her and has sustained her in some of the most difficult situations that she has faced in her life. "Mother Mary has suffused me with her divine love, and since that 'end of the world' vision that I received as a child, I have been a student of prophecy and the 'end-time' warnings."

Mother Mary's Love Is for Everyone

Regardless of one's religious background or spiritual yearnings, as Lori Jean Flory reminds us, Mother Mary comes forth with love, reverence, faith, and respect of a mother to wrap her arms completely around the Earth and around each one of us.

At this unique moment in history, Annie Kirkwood says, Mary is showing up all over the world as a nurturing maternal figure to demonstrate to the entire planet that God is also loving as a mother is loving: "People are hungering for a mother-grandmother kind of love. The great masses are tired of an angry father God. They now desire a loving mother."

And why *now* at this particular tick of the cosmic clock in the passing parade of time is Mother Mary making appearances on a global basis? "Because it is time!" she told Rev. Pam Wade: "Humankind is ready."

Mother Mary explained to Beverly Hale Watson that another reason why she and other heavenly beings appear to humans is to provide proof that there is an eternal existence beyond physical death.

Although the planet may be in for some difficult times, many of our revelators were advised by Mother Mary that prayer can alleviate the fear and chaos of the fast-approaching times of transformation and transition. As Mary told Brenda Montgomery, "You must pray for healing. In prayer all things are possible. Even Mother Earth can be released from the torments of her changes. Enough prayer can change the universe."

And while we pray and seek guidance, the Divine Mother warned the messenger known as Liberty that this is a time when great discernment should be used. "False prophets are everywhere. You must use discernment. You must stay in your own truth and not someone else's. There is no point in searching for truth if you never look within and find your own."

At the same time, Mary, speaking through Rev. Pam Wade, stated that the workers of the light of truth and love are the instruments of growth and enlightenment on the Earth. "Your hearts and minds are in the unity of creation. Your hearts and souls cry out to put away falsity."

Allow Mother Mary and Divine Revelation to Enter Your Life

In pondering the question of whether or not we should deliberately seek and encourage a revelatory experience with Mother Mary or any other holy figure, we would probably agree with our friend Dr. Bruce Wrightsman, who holds doctorates in both physics and religion, when he said, "I think the revelatory experience can be sought, but I don't think it can be manipulated. Everything depends upon the quality of mind and heart that one brings to life, and that's one of the imponderable things that makes it impossible for us to predict who's going to receive revelation and who isn't."

Dr. Wrightsman went on to say that he thought we could make ourselves more receptive to the revelatory experience. "I think we do have that responsibility to make ourselves more receptive through prayer, meditation, worship—which, if it doesn't create the conditions for revelation, at least offers the opportunity for God to get through."

Another longtime friend, Fr. Ed Cleary, a Roman Catholic priest, offered his advice that the best way to encourage the revelatory experience is steadily "to cultivate contemplation—the condition of stillness or quiet of all the outer principles, powers, and acts of mind, emotion, sense, and body so that the inner principles and acts of soul, spirit, and God can manifest, or surface, in consciousness.

"Contemplation offers the best climate for the revelatory fruit. Whatever happens in this condition has the most chance of being genuine—though the outer ego still has to express it, and this necessarily causes a loss of degree of its authenticity."

Dr. Martin Marty, a well-known and highly respected theologian at the University of Chicago, commented that it was hard for him to see how a person could be in a religious tradition, as he is in the Christian tradition, and say that once upon a time we encouraged prophecy and listening and speaking and now we don't. "It is itself a very heavy theological commitment to suggest that once there was a Holy Spirit and now the world is abandoned to itself.

"I must confess that I am usually skeptical about what comes up, and, in biblical terms, I *test* the Spirit. . . . In general, though, insofar as revelation is a theological translation of a code word for altered states of consciousness—or an enlarged range of human experience—I would just have to say, Why not?"

Diane Kennedy Pike, widow of Bishop James Pike, told us that based on her study of the early Christians and the Dead Sea scrolls, we should first seek to purify and order our own lives in the physical dimension and in the emotional and mental dimensions so that we can do all we can to make ourselves as perfect an instrument as we can for spirit.

"Second," she continued, "we should seek to alter ourselves to God for the experience of unity with Him—or we should seek to achieve the higher states of consciousness so that we can experience unity with the cosmic forces or with the whole universe, or however the experience comes."

Diane wisely cautions against our seeking a particular message or a new understanding, for "our mind will almost inevitably get involved in the formulating of what we would like to come by way of revelation. We have somehow set up a precondition.

"My feeling is that we should seek higher states of consciousness or union with God or the gift of the Holy Spirit, but we should not set up preconditions as to how that gift should manifest. . . . It says in the New Testament that the Spirit moves where it will, and I don't think we have any say over that. . . . I feel that we should aspire to the highest level of spiritual consciousness that is possible in our lives— and then wait to be given whatever gifts God chooses to give us and not have any predetermined ideas about that.

"If we receive revelation or new understanding or new messages from some higher beings, then we should consider this a great gift and a great responsibility, because those who are given those gifts are expected to do something great with them."

Throughout this book we have heard Mother Mary speak repeatedly of the power of love and prayer. And even though the revelators and healers whom she has chosen may not have truly understood the limitless dimensions of

Mother Mary's holy splendor, their prayers, love, and deeds were magnified by the power of her divine maternal energy.

Surely, we must keep our own light strong as we walk our individual life pathway and fulfill our mission here on Earth. With the Divine Mother's loving hand in our own, we will draw upon her strength to become more aware, more compassionate, more light-filled, and more expressive of unconditional love. After all, she is our Holy Mother, and she will not deny us that which we most need—the progression from our old, physical selves on Earth to our rightful place as more highly developed spiritual beings in the Heavenly Kingdom.

Selected Bibliography

Armstrong, Karen. *The Gospel According to Woman*. Garden City, N.Y.: Anchor Press/Doubleday, 1987.

Cranston, Ruth. *The Miracle of Lourdes*. New York: McGraw-Hill, 1955.

Crockett, Arthur. *Secret Prophecy of Fatima Revealed*. New York: Global Communications, 1982.

Delaney, John J., ed. *A Woman Clothed with the Sun*. Garden City, N.Y.: Doubleday, 1961.

De Lubac, Henri. *The Eternal Feminine*. New York: Harper and Row, 1971.

Fox, Robin Lane. *Pagans and Christians*. New York: Alfred A. Knopf, 1989.

Goddard, Lester O. *Prophets and Prophecies: 1996–2002*. Pittsburgh: Dorrance Publishing, 1996.

Hastings, Arthur. *With the Tongues of Men and Angels*. Ft. Worth, Tex.: Holt, Rinehart, Winston, 1991.

Hayford, Jack. *The Mary Miracle*. Ventura, Cal.: Gospel Light, 1994.

Kirkwood, Annie. *Mary's Message of Hope*. Nevada City, Cal.: Blue Dolphin Publishing, 1995.

————. *Mary's Message to the World*. New York: Putnam, 1991.

Kirkwood, Annie, and Byron Kirkwood. *Messages to Our Family*. Nevada City, Cal.: Blue Dolphin Publishing, 1994.

Kirkwood, Byron. *Survival Guide for the New Millennium*. Nevada City, Cal.: Blue Dolphin Publishing, 1993.

Laurentin, Rene. *Our Lord and Our Lady in Scottsdale*. Milford, Ohio: Faith Publishing, 1992.

Matthews, Caitlin. *Sophia, Goddess of Wisdom*. London: HarperCollins/Aquarian Press, 1992.

McDannell, Colleen, and Bernhard Lang. *Heaven—A History*. New York: Vintage Books, 1990.

Neumann, Erich. *The Great Mother*. Princeton, N.J.: Princeton University Press, 1974.

Nicholson, Shirley, ed. *The Goddess Re-Awakening*. Wheaten, Ill.: Theosophical Publishing House, 1989.

Robinson, James M., ed. *The Nag Hammadi Library*. New York: Harper and Row, 1978.

Sjoo, Monica, and Barbara Mor. *The Great Cosmic Mother*. New York: Harper and Row, 1987.

Steiger, Brad. *The Gods of Aquarius*. New York: Harcourt Brace Jovanovich, 1977.

————. *Revelation: The Divine Fire*. Englewood Cliffs, N.J.: Prentice Hall, 1973.

Young, Samuel H. *Psychic Children*. Garden City, N.Y.: Doubleday, 1977.

Zimdars-Swartz, Sandral. *Encountering Mary*. New York: Avon Books, 1992.

For Additional Information

Annie and Byron Kirkwood
Route One—Box 100
Bunch, OK 74931

Rev. Jayne M. Howard
Angel Heights
P.O. Box 95
Upperco, MD 21155

Marti Betz
Divine Mother Reprints
922 Melvin Road
Annapolis, MD 21403

Rev. Pam Wade and Rev. Marie Trump
Life's Pathway
Route 1, Box 127A
Leavenworth, IN 47137

Clarisa Bernhardt
P.O. Box 669
Winnipeg, Manitoba R3C 2K3
Canada

Brenda Montgomery
Transformational Arts
1860 12th Street
Los Osos, CA 93402

Beverly Hale Watson
Sevenfold Peace Foundation
4704 Quail Ridge Drive
Charlotte, NC 28227

Liberty
c/o Sevenfold Peace Foundation
4704 Quail Ridge Drive
Charlotte, NC 28227

Lori Jean and Charles Flory
P.O. Box 1328
Conifer, CO 80433

Lorraine Darr
c/o Timewalker Productions
P.O. Box 434
Forest City, IA 50436

The Bulletin: Association of Marian Helpers
Eden Hill
Stockbridge, MA 01263

Omega New Age Directory
6418 S. 39th Avenue
Phoenix, AZ 85041

Gnosis
Lumen Foundation
347 Dolores Street, Suite 305
San Francisco, CA 94110

Brad Steiger and Sherry Hansen Steiger
To receive a copy of the Steiger Questionnaire of Mystical, Paranormal, and UFO Experiences, plus a catalog of tapes and books, send a stamped, self-addressed envelope to Timewalker Productions, P.O. Box 434, Forest City, IA 50436.